Cheng Tzu's Thirteen Treatises on T'ai Chi Ch'uan

By
Professor
Cheng Man Ch'ing

Translated by
Benjamin Pang Jeng Lo
and
Martin Inn

North Atlantic Books
Berkeley, California

Published by
North Atlantic Books
P.O. Box 12327
Berkeley, California 94712

Cover and book design by Paula Morrison
Typeset by Classic Typography
Printed in the United States of America

Cheng Tzu's Thirteen Treatises on T'ai Chi Ch'uan is sponsored by the Society for the Study of Native Arts and Sciences, a nonprofit educational corporation whose goals are to develop an educational and cross-cultural perspective linking various scientific, social, and artistic fields; to nurture a holistic view of arts, sciences, humanities, and healing; and to publish and distribute literature on the relationship of mind, body, and nature.

Library of Congress Cataloging-in-Publication Data

Cheng, Man-ch'ing
  Cheng-Tzu's thirteen treatises on t'ai chi ch'uan
  Translation of: Cheng-tzu t'ai chi ch'üan shih san p'ien.
  1. T'ai chi ch'uan—Addresses, essay, lectures.
I. Lo, Benjamin Pang Jeng. II. Inn, Martin. III. Title. IV. Title:
Cheng-Tzu's 13 treatises on t'ai chi ch'uan. V. Title: Thirteen
treatises on t'ai chi ch'uan
GV505.C45813 1985   796.8'155   85-15218
ISBN 0-938190-45-8

Professor Cheng Man Ch'ing

Acknowledgements

We would like to express our thanks to Madame Cheng Man-ch'ing for her encouragement and permission to translate this book, and for also writing a preface.

In translating a book of such complexity it takes the collective energy of many people who contribute their ideas, edit and proof read the manuscript. We would like to thank Robert W. Smith, Jim Hill, John Lang, Warren Conner, John Ladd, Will Poulsen, Father Arthur Swain, S.J., Classics Department, University of San Francisco, Andrew Main, Susan Foe, William Haught, and Mr. Liu Si-heng in Taiwan. Special thanks to Richard Grossinger for reworking the whole manuscript.

Contents

Introduction
by Madame Cheng

When my late husband Man-ching was very young his body was extremely weak. Although his physical condition was poor he was very clever and studied hard. At the age of twenty he had already accepted the position as professor of literature at universities in Peiping and Shanghai, and he was also the head of the Chinese Traditional Painting Department of the Fine Arts Academy in Shanghai. Because of his heavy teaching responsibilities and social commitments with other poets, he contracted a lung disease. His condition steadily worsened and the medical doctors were unable to help him. Fortunately by that time his friends had introduced him to the great T'ai Chi Ch'uan master Yang Cheng-fu and he became the last disciple of Master Yang. For six years he studied with Master Yang everyday and his body became healthy and strong. My husband deeply felt that T'ai Chi Ch'uan could benefit everyone, and he was anxious to spread this art to all. He followed the proverb, "The good doctor cures people before they become ill." At that time in China very few people practiced this art and there wasn't even a reference to T'ai Chi Ch'uan in bookstores.

My husband wrote this book in 1947 for the sake of teaching convenience. He put his many years of insights and experience into it. However, at that time the country was not at peace and the book was not able to be published. In 1949 we moved to Taiwan Province. Because Taiwan was previously occupied by the Japanese for fifty years my husband felt that the younger generation had been alienated from Chinese culture too long and he therefore felt a greater responsibility to spread this art. During that time the mayor of Taipei, Mr. Yu Mi-chien, had the same strong feeling and he encouraged my husband. In November, 1950, my husband published this book and it quickly became popular everywhere. During these years my husband tried to translate this book into English, but it was difficult to find someone good in both English and Chinese. It was, however, even more difficult to find someone who also knew T'ai Chi Ch'uan well, and therefore this book was left untranslated.

There are unscrupulous people who have made translations and published them. I worry that they didn't know my husband's original meaning and therefore translated this book subjectively, or that their translations were limited by their own abilities in T'ai Chi Ch'uan. If errors exist in their translations then it will defeat our original purpose and greatly mislead the readers.

My husband's student Lo Pang-jeng studied T'ai Chi Ch'uan with him since 1949. In the last 10 years Pang-jeng has taught this art throughout the United States and Europe. I had asked Pang-jeng many times to fulfill his teacher's ambition by translating this book into English to help future T'ai Chi Ch'uan practitioners. Recently Pang-jeng and his good friend Martin Inn finished this translation and they asked me to write the above introduction.

Cheng, Ting Wei-chuang
Republic of China
Houston, Texas
March 1985

Introduction
by Benjamin Pang-jeng Lo

In the summer of 1974 I came to the United States to teach T'ai Chi Ch'uan in San Francisco. Up till now most of my students who have studied with me do not know Chinese. In my classes I often quote and explain from the *T'ai Chi Ch'uan Classics* and these depended completely on my oral interpretation. For a long time my students asked me to translate the *Classics* into English so that they could study T'ai Chi Ch'uan by themselves. Therefore with my friends I translated the *Classics* into English, which became the *Essence of T'ai Chi Ch'uan*, and it was published in 1977.

At the same time, while I was teaching, I also quoted and gave instruction from my late teacher Professor Cheng Man-ch'ing's book, *Cheng-tzu Thirteen Treatises on T'ai Chi Ch'uan*. My students also wanted me to translate this into English. My American classmates had the very same idea but felt that this was a big task and dreaded it.

During the last ten years I often returned to Taiwan where my old classmates also encouraged me to do this translation. I always answered, "The well is deep and my rope too short. My ability is not up to the task." Madame Cheng also often encouraged me. She felt that because I had studied with the Professor for the longest time of all his students in Taiwan and deeply felt the kindness from his teaching, I should try to do my best to dispel bad translations and twisted meanings of my teacher's book. This translation would also prevent the passing down of misconceptions to future T'ai Chi Ch'uan practitioners. Furthermore, if we desire to spread this art accurately to future generations, it is necessary to translate

11

this book. After I listened to Madame Cheng's words I was moved to re-read this book. In the meantime I talked with my friend Martin Inn who happily consented to undertake the translation with me. We took two years to complete the task.

I feel that over the years I have received many benefits from this book. If this translation can help future T'ai Chi Ch'uan practitioners then it would be a good thing! The work of translating is not easy. Even if Martin and I have done our best with the help of our classmates, friends and students, I fear that there might still be some mistakes. I hope that our readers will correct our mistakes.

Benjamin Pang-jeng Lo
San Francisco, California

The Biography of Man-Jan

When I was young I studied at Mt. Kuang-lu; I visited many old temples in my leisure time. In Hai Hui Temple I met a monk eighty years old, a native of Hopei Province. Past noon, he did not eat. His facial color was like that of a child's. He was a master of the martial arts. Behind his monastery was Mt. Wu Lao Feng. In the cliffs the *shiherh* herb (parmelia), grows. Others could not get it but he always managed to. He would hold on to the pine trees and vines and move quickly like a monkey or bird such was the lightness of his body.

Later I visited Mt. Ch'ing-cheng and met the Taoist priest Hung in Ch'ang Tao Kuan Temple. He was about seventy. At night I saw him sitting on the wooden bed, without blanket or pillow, meditating. Hung said he had been doing this for forty years. His beard and hair were all black. His voice was clear and distinct, and its sound lingered.

In my life I have met only a few exceptional people. Including "Whiskers" Man they total three. When "Whiskers" was a child he liked to jump and climb about. Whatever he liked he did. He was a smart, sensitive child and quickly reacted to whatever happened. One day while he was playing under a dangerous wall it collapsed, injuring his head. He was unconscious for a long time and after he regained consciousness his mental faculties were impaired. Later he contracted a pulmonary disease. After studying T'ai Chi Ch'uan, he recovered his mental faculties, and his body got stronger. After a few years, even strong people seemed weak compared to him. In his studies of Chinese medicine, painting, and calligraphy he reached the highest level. He also liked visiting scenic mountains with their deep gorges. Danger did not deter him — once he met a tiger but was not frightened because he was internally strong and his mind was calm.

He was an excellent Chinese herbalist. He felt that although medicine could cure disease, T'ai Chi Ch'uan could prevent it. If a country's people are weak how can they protect their homeland? Even if they have the most modern weapons how can they use them effectively? Without strong people to use them, having weapons is like having no weapons at all. When Confucius taught people the Six Arts (propriety, music, archery, charioteering, writing, mathematics) he insisted that without the training of archery and charioteering no one could learn the mental discipline of the other four arts.

The daily lives of the people of China are different from those of Westerners. Therefore, they must have an exercise suited to them to make their bodies strong. Cheng held the opinion that this would best be T'ai Chi Ch'uan. When he met people he never tired of speaking to them about T'ai Chi Ch'uan. He taught this art to thousands of students, each according to his own talents. Yet he feared that by personal teaching alone he would not be able to spread this art to everyone. Therefore, he wrote *Cheng Tzu's Thirteen Treatises on T'ai Chi Ch'uan* to bring out the secrets of what he had discovered from former practitioners together with his own insights. *Sun Tzu's Thirteen Treatises (The Art of War)* was passed down from generation to generation. Whether Sun himself actually wrote it or not, nonetheless no one dares disregard its words. "Whiskers" used this *Thirteen Treatises* to name his own T'ai Chi Ch'uan book. Did he intend thereby to offer his book as a modern textbook for those who desired to train soldiers for warfare to co-ordinate political strategy? Perhaps. The world is unsettled and our nation is not at peace. "Whiskers" turned his atten-

14

tion to these conditions. He was a great man compared with those who stayed in old temples and remote mountains, who preferrred to seek quietness and protect themselves rather than participate in the country's destiny or the rise and fall of the world.

Man-Jan's native town was Yung Chia. His family name was Cheng and his given name was Yue. His other name was Man-ch'ing. Long ago Chu Ko-kung praised Kuan Chuang-miaos' whiskers saying "Yours are incomparable with others." Today I take this idea using "Whiskers" to name Cheng's biography.

Min Hsiao-chi
Kiangsi Province,
Chiu Chiang City

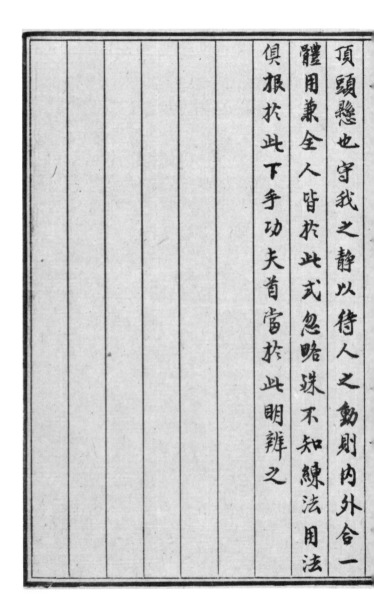

頂頭懸也守我之靜以待人之動則內外合一

體用兼全人皆於此式忽略殊不知練法用法

俱根於此下手功夫首當於此明辨之

A page of Professor Cheng's calligraphy from his original

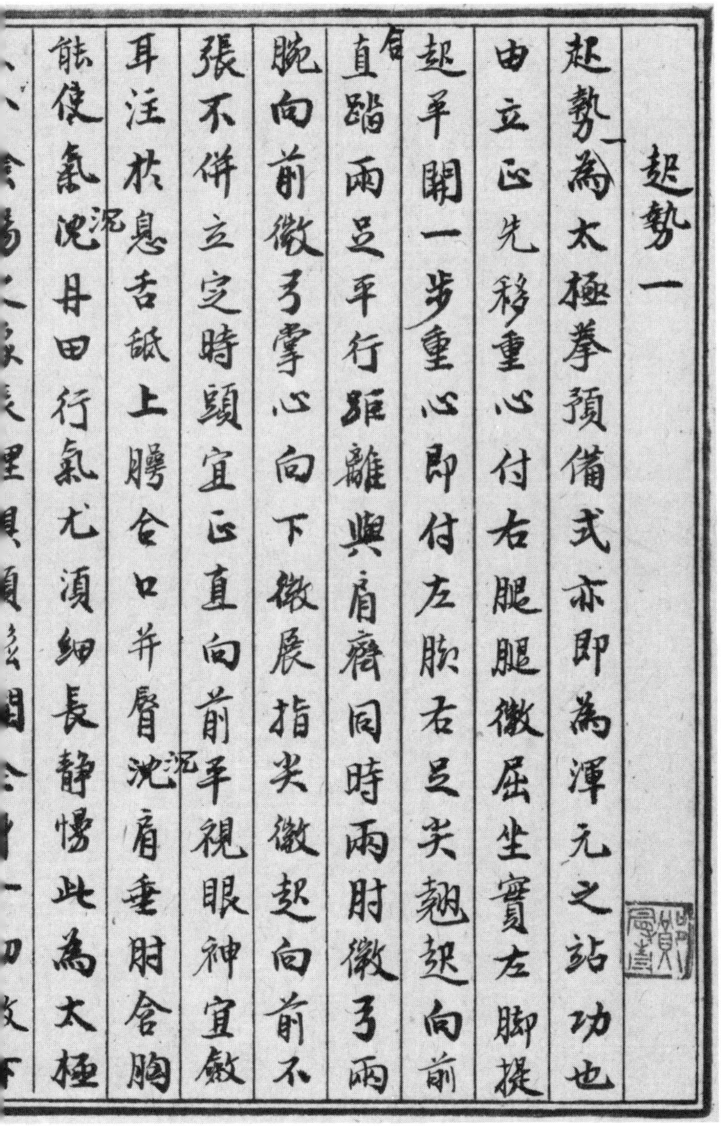

起勢一

起勢為太極拳預備式亦即為渾元之站功也

由立正先移重心付右腿腿微屈坐實左腳提

起平開一步重心即付左胲右呂关翹趻向前

直蹈兩呂平行距離與肩膺同時兩肘微弓兩

腕向前微弓掌心向下微展指尖微起向前不

張不併立定時頭宜正直向前平視眼神宜斂

耳注狀息舌舐上腭合口并脣沈肩垂肘含胸

能使氣沈丹田行氣尤須細長靜慢此為太極

manuscript (translated on page 114 of this book.)

鄭子太極拳十三篇 卷上

Cheng Tzu's Thirteen Treatises on T'ai Chi Ch'uan

Section I

Treatise One

Explanation of the Name and Definition

Martial arts have been developed to increase both wisdom and bravery. In Chinese Philosophy *T'ai Chi* is the mother of *yin* and *yang*. There is nothing it does not contain. From this primordial *T'ai Chi*, comes the name of our martial art. The *Book of Changes* states that *T'ai Chi* gives birth to the *Liang I* (the Two Primordial Powers), *yin* and *yang*. Extreme *yin* produces *yang*, and extreme *yang* produces *yin*. In the alternation of hard and soft, and movement and stillness, each is applied to its limit.

People who are fond of fighting like to use martial arts to do battle. Losing or winning is determined by the relative level of martial skills. These types invariably use hard force to strike and quick techniques to control opponents. This is the extreme limit of *yang*, and the extreme limit of hardness. If one uses hardness to resist, then both sides are certain to lose or be injured. This is not the way of a great master. Therefore, when others use hardness, I use softness to neutralize it. When others use movement to attack, I use stillness and wait for the attack and neutralize it. Extreme softness and stillness is

21

the fruition of *yin*. When extreme *yang* encounters extreme *yin*, the *yang* will always be defeated. Of this Lao-Tzu said, "The soft and pliable will defeat the hard and strong." Therefore I say, "To learn T'ai Chi Ch'uan, it is first necessary to learn to invest in loss." When one learns to invest in loss, [the loss] will polarize into its opposite and be transformed into the greatest profit. For example, the teeth are hard and the tongue is soft. When the teeth and tongue do not properly meet, the tongue will be temporarily useless; but because the teeth are hard, they will eventually be broken and because the tongue is pliable, it will remain. This demonstrates my meaning.

There has never been a person who has studied the martial arts who did not first desire to win and gain the advantage. Now when I say, "Learn to invest in loss," who is willing to do this? To invest in loss is to permit others to use force to attack while you don't use even the slightest force to defend yourself. On the contrary, you lead an opponent's force away so that it is useless. Then when you counter, any opponent will be thrown out a great distance. The Classics refer to this as "*tung chin*" (understanding strength) and say: "After you understand the *chin*, the more practice, the more skill." When you can enact whatever you think, you will then obtain the greatest benefit. This is the subtlety and application of T'ai Chi Ch'uan and it conforms to the principle of the [philosophical] *T'ai Chi*. It was first transmitted from Chang San-feng down through many generations. I received the secrets passed by my teacher, Professor Yang Cheng-fu; then I understood that the use of T'ai Chi

Ch'uan is completely based on the principles of *T'ai Chi* and that *yin* and *yang* create each other and that hardness and softness overcome each other. Anyone can see this truth. There is a good reason to use the title "*T'ai Chi*" for this martial art. T'ai Chi Ch'uan can not only destroy hardness but can also be used to control movement. It is the premier martial art. It helps the weak to become strong, the sick to recover, and the timid to become brave. Its practice strengthens the body, the race, and the country. Those who deal with national and civil affairs should not neglect this.

Treatise Two

Understanding the Occult and the Physical

The name *"T'ai Chi"* comes from the *Book of Changes*. It also comes from the classics of Chinese traditional medicine and of Taoism. The theory and function of *T'ai Chi* principles are found everywhere. Confucius said, "It embodies the scope of the interaction of Heaven and Earth." Its principles are fully comprised in *yin* and *yang*, the transformation of *ch'i* is contained in the Five Elements. This is the matrix of Chinese culture and philosophy. It would be ridiculous to talk about *T'ai Chi* without discussing *yin* and *yang* and the Five Elements. If you get rid of *yin* and *yang* and the Five Elements and try to discuss Chinese philosophy, Chinese medicine, and Taoism, it is like getting rid of arithmetic and algebra and then trying to discuss mathematics. Today's science has already progressed from the advent of electricity to the Atomic Age. Can these be separated from the function of *yin* and *yang*? T'ai Chi Ch'uan is consistent with both philosophy and science. Its theory is entirely based on philosophic principles; yet it realizes those principles in a way that satisfies the standards of science. All of this can be confirmed by its actual substance and application and is not a matter of opinion.

The *Classics* of T'ai Chi Ch'uan are wonderful and their execution extraordinary. Here I will try to make it easier by using a small portion to help explain the whole. In talking about exercise the *Classics* state: "Use the mind to mobilize the *ch'i*, use the *ch'i* to mobilize the body." When the body is mobilized, then there is movement. This is similar to a train or ship using steam power to move and different from exercising by moving just one isolated part of the body. The *Classics* further state, "Relax the inner abdomen, then the whole body is light and agile," and "Use four ounces to deflect a thousand pounds." This is all related to the nonuse of force. Not using force means not receiving the force of another's attack. Not receiving force is controlled by me and is the substance of the art. It is easy. "Use four ounces to deflect 1000 pounds" is the function. How can you "use four ounces to deflect 1000 pounds"? It is accomplished by causing the weight at the opponent's center of gravity to be off balance. Then, even if you don't use four ounces to deflect him, he will topple anyway.

Can this be confirmed by philosophy or science? The *Classics* say, "The *ch'i* permeates into the bone and becomes pure steel. There is nothing hard that it cannot destroy." We need to explain this further. In the Spring of 1929, Mr. Ts'ao, who had examined Marconi's theory, studied T'ai Chi Ch'uan with me. I told him to sink the *ch'i* to the *tan t'ien*. He asked me, "What is the use of that?" I said, "Sinking *ch'i* has benefits, but these are less than the benefits of having the mind and the *ch'i* together and staying in the *tan t'ien*." He said, "I would like to know more details." I replied by telling him that a person's abdomen stores up much water. It is similar to our earth having too much water. Excess rain may saturate the land. The minor harm is that dams break, and the major harm is that flooding occurs. When the body contains too much water, major illnesses will develop such as edema, jaundice, or paralysis. Lesser ailments will also occur: too much sputum, ring worms, rashes, and many types of diseases of the lungs, spleen, stomach, and intestines. To prevent illnesses from excess water in the body it is necessary to exercise. This activity can be compared to that of the Legendary Yu who was in charge of the waterworks in Ancient China and cleared the waterways to help the water flow. However, this is nothing compared to the action of the sun evaporating the water from the earth. If the human body could do this it would be wonderful. Yet, the mind and the *ch'i* welling together in the *tan t'ien* can have a similar result. Why? Because sinking the *ch'i* to the *tan t'ien* is like putting warm air in a clay pot: it dispels the cold wet air. If the *ch'i* can stay with the mind, this is like putting fire under the clay pot and making the water boil. Gradually it becomes steam. In this manner the water will not cause health problems, but, on the contrary, will help to circulate the blood and bestow a great benefit. Mr. Ts'ao exclaimed, "Formerly, I thought that philosophy was just philosophy. Now I know that today's philosophy will be tomorrow's science." Then I further stated that when the *ch'i* permeates the bone, there will be pure steel. This happens when the *ch'i* moves from the *tan t'ien* through the coccyx and reaches the spine. It surprised Mr. Ts'ao, so he visited a Western doctor and asked about it. The doctor said that he had heard of something similar to sinking the *ch'i* to the *tan t'ien* and that recently a French doctor dissected a cadaver and discovered a bag-like structure in the abdomen between the membranes of the intestine. He said that only in athletes is the skin of this bag thicker than in others. When the bag is struck, it can resist blows. The French doctor said, "Maybe this is what is referred to by the Chinese as the *tan t'ien*. But there is no direct route from the coccyx to the spine."

Later Mr. Ts'ao returned to talk with me and told me what had occurred. I said that this doctor's knowledge was limited by his personal experience and that apparently he did not care to know more. That athletes have this thick bag and that it can resist blows is correct because this bag contains *ch'i*. When the *ch'i* is increasingly accumulated, it then passes through to the membranes. These membranes will be thicker than in other people, and the bag will be able to resist blows. But this is because the *ch'i* reaches the membranes and not because the bag itself can take the blows. If there were an overt pathway from the coccyx to the spine then it would be common knowledge and would not require further study.

When the *ch'i* and mind stay together in the *tan t'ien*, this not only transforms the water to *ch'i* but also transforms the semen into *ch'i*. The heat generated from the transformation of semen is like electric power. Electricity can be conducted through water, earth, and metal. The heat from the *ch'i* can also be conducted

27

through the spine. The coccyx and spine comprise an area of multiple vertebrae. Although there is no direct route between *tan t'ien*, coccyx, and spine, there is a sequence of points with gaps in between them, covered by ligaments, cartilage, and membranes. The heat that comes from the semen *ch'i* and the heart fire gently warm these points. This process is ramified by the *ch'i* from the *tan t'ien*, which makes this heat go through the coccyx and up the spine until it reaches the headtop and spreads to the four limbs. The warm *ch'i* fills up the bones and remains inside until the semen *ch'i* forms a sticky substance. This sticky substance becomes marrow and adheres to the inside of the bones like the plating of nickel or gold. This is what the ancients meant when they measured one's daily enhancement by the thickness of a sheet of paper. When the marrow is built up over a long period of time the bones will be strong. Such is the process by which the bones become the pure hardness that can overcome anything.

All of this effect is based on *yin* and *yang* and the Five Elements. We can provide evidence of it. The weight of my teacher's arm was ten times greater than most person's. When he used it to hit others they were always injured. I am not as skilled as my teacher, but my arm is still several times heavier than others'. The tiger's bone is different from other animals' because the inside of his bone is filled with marrow like a rock and there are no gaps. Such is the basis of his strength. This further reconciles T'ai Chi Ch'uan with philosophy and science.

Mr. Ts'ao exclaimed, "Wonderful! T'ai Chi Ch'uan

originated from philosophy and is confirmed by science. I believe what you say." I told him that I was only discussing transforming the *ching* to *ch'i* and cultivating the *ch'i* to enrich the brain. There is further cultivation of the *ch'i* to transform it into spirit and of the spirit to return to emptiness. Then you can reach the supernatural. But I have not reached this level. Mr. Ts'ao said, "That is enough! Hearing this I can understand it. The principle exists and its consequences must follow. There will be sure confirmation of its truth in the future."

Treatise Three

Developing the Ch'i to Attain Suppleness

The special quality of T'ai Chi Ch'uan is its ability to sink the *ch'i* to the *tan t'ien*. This is the first degree of what Lao-Tzu referred to as "developing the *ch'i* to reach suppleness". Lao-Tzu said, "Those who are pliable and weak are alive and those who are hard and strong are dead." From this we can see that the way to cultivate life is to be supple. If you desire to be supple, you must first develop the *ch'i*. The perfect place to develop the *ch'i* is in the *tan t'ien*. When the *ch'i* can sink to the *tan t'ien*, it is what the *Book of Changes* calls water and fire "After Completion;" it consists of the meeting of the two trigrams ☵ *K'an* and *Li*. Both trigrams have strong natures and are the antithesis of pliability and weakness.

Li is the fire of the heart flaming above. *K'an* represents the water of the kidneys, and it moistens the lower body. The movement of the trigrams is in opposite directions. About seventy percent of the abdomen is water. There are then two kinds of fire: primary and assisting. In the "Latter Heaven" arrangement of the Eight Trigrams in the *Book of Changes*, *Li* is the primary fire, the fire of the heart; it is the substantial fire. In the *Classic of Internal Medicine* the Gate of Life is the assisting, or insubstantial, fire. These two kinds of fires can penetrate the internal organs and every part of the body. If there is too much fire, however, it will cause illness. What Chinese traditional medicine calls "having fire" Western medicine calls inflammation. Yet, clearly, even if the fire spreads throughout the whole body it can never overcome the accumulated water. Without water our body would dry up, and without fire we would have poor digestion. We must have water and fire in our body but neither in excess. If you let the fire naturally flame up and the water accumulate unchecked below, you will have the condition the *Book of Changes* calls "Before Completion." ☲ How can this state of affairs be maintained for very long? Lao-tzu studied and interpreted the *Book of Changes*; reading between the lines, he said, "Develop the *ch'i* to reach suppleness." That is, sink the *ch'i* to the *tan t'ien* and keep it there with the mind. The *tan t'ien* is like a stove. The heart is in the stove and the water is on top. The fire warms the water and prevents it from sinking downward to cause maladies. Meanwhile, there is the benefit that the water evaporates. Water helps control the fire when the water is on top and the fire is below. This prevents the fire from causing problems by burning upward. Concurrently, there is the benefit of nurturing warmth. This is called "After Completion." ☵ If *K'an* and *Li* are properly balanced as in "After Completion," then the generation of *ch'i* to attain suppleness is successful. Do not allow water and fire to work at counterpurposes.

When fire and water are in the state known as "After Completion," why do we still have to intensify the *ch'i* to become supple? Because there are numerous benefits from developing the *ch'i*. Here I will enumerate just some:

1. The *tan t'ien* is only a bag of *ch'i*. If the *ch'i* doesn't sink into the *tan t'ien*, the bag will not be open and therefore cannot function. Even if you mobilize the heart fire to the *tan t'ien*, it will not work.

2. If the mind and *ch'i* do not stay together and if they wander aimlessly, you cannot pay attention to the *ch'i*. How do you know whether the *ch'i* reaches the *tan t'ien* or not? To develop the *ch'i* and sink it to the *tan t'ien* you must keep the *ch'i* with the mind. Then you will realize suppleness. The *Classics* say, "The mind mobilizes the *ch'i* and the *ch'i* mobilizes the body. The *ch'i* spreads throughout the whole body." First, you must sink the *ch'i* to the *tan t'ien*; then you can talk about mobilizing the *ch'i*. This is only a small aspect of the process of developing the *ch'i*.

What is the benefit to your body of intensifying the *ch'i*? Lao-tzu explained this when he said, "To develop the *ch'i* is to become supple like an infant." The infant is the young human sprout which will grow up. It is pliable and weak like the seedling of a plant. From the time the infant grows up and becomes a young person, from that time until he grows old, he will never again have this vitality; he will become hard and strong. When wood is strong, it can be broken easily and is not far from death. If people are in this condition, how can they become like an infant again? The infant's body is pure *yang*. Being pure *yang* it has marvelous *ch'i*. When the *ch'i* is marvelous, then the blood is full. When the blood is full, then the vessels are supple. Supple blood vessels are unique to infants. A person who is close to death but still hopes to return to being a child can accomplish this only by developing the *ch'i* to become supple. To save ourselves in the midst of crashing waves and to regain life requires "Water and Fire After Completion."

How can this be done? We find the answer in the beginning of the *Classics* where it says, "The *ch'i* should be *excited*, the *shen* should be internally gathered," and at the end of the *Classics* where it says, "Throughout the body, the *i* (mind) relies on the *ching shen* (spirit), not on the *ch'i* (breath). If *i* relied on the *ch'i*, it would become stagnant. If there is *ch'i*, there is no *li* (external strength). If there is no *ch'i*, there is pure steel." The word "excited" means that my *ch'i* vibrates with the air. This is a higher level than mobilizing the *ch'i* to spread it throughout the whole body. The term "gather the spirit" is a step beyond developing the *ch'i*. If one develops the *ch'i* to the highest level through practice, then one can transform the semen into *ch'i*. This, however, is still not the pure *yang* level. Reaching the level where "*i* (mind) depends on the *ching shen* (spirit) not on the *ch'i*" and where "there is no *ch'i*, there is pure steel" is perfect; in it, one has attained the pure *yang*. This conforms to Lao-tzu's theory of "developing the *ch'i* to reach suppleness." If one can achieve this, then one can eliminate illness. Then longevity is nothing.

Treatise Four

Changing the
Temperament

Studying the works of the Sages, seriously following them, carefully questioning them, striving for clarity in the resolution of the problems they posed, I made the *Six Classics* my *vade mecum*. I believe that these *Classics* can without any doubt change a person's temperament. But I have never heard that studying T'ai Chi Ch'uan can change one's temperament. I have practiced T'ai Chi Ch'uan for almost thirty years, the latter twenty-one of them uninterrupted, and yet I am not sure how much it changed me. I would like to recount some of my experiences.

When I was young I had a sense of justice, but recklessly disregarded the consequences of my actions. I had the ambition to study hard to reach the highest level, but my physical energy was low. Consequently I interrupted my practice several times and did not accomplish much. Now I have already surpassed the age when P'eng Chü had white hair and the time when K'ung Ming ate less food. What can I say? Immortality, wealth, and respect are not what I aspire to. I desire only to hear the true Tao (of Confucius); then I'll be satisfied. Therefore, I don't dare abandon myself and waste my life.

After practicing T'ai Chi Ch'uan for twenty-nine years, I discovered that it could raise the spirit, increase strength, and eliminate illness. Now, whatever I do, I have endurance and this has checked the habitual interruption of my studies. Even if I don't have perfect peace and calm within, I have eliminated my reckless and uncaring attitude. I do not expect the change of temperament to be as great a change as a thorn becoming an orchid or an owl becoming a phoenix, but I think that if your spirit and physical energy are low, then even if you are young, you will be weak, and even if you are strong, you will be sick. When you become weak and sick, you will not be able to improve yourself even if you want to. You cannot effectively discuss change of temperament. If you cannot improve yourself for the benefit of yourself and your family, you will betray your country just as corrupt government officials do. You will commit these acts even though you know they are wrong. There must be a reason—it is because your body is weak. I know many who would rather live in dishonor than die in honor. In half of these people their physical energy and spirit cannot support them. Therefore, the discussion of change of temperament pertains to ordinary people who can improve themselves to become superior people. If the ordinary person slips backwards, he becomes only inferior. So I conclude that the question of whether or not T'ai Chi Ch'uan can change someone's temperament must await someone wiser to answer it.

陸
地
游
泳

Treatise Five

Swimming on Land

Today most people realize that there is no more supple exercise than swimming. Although we know that the best way to exercise is to be supple, swimming has many shortcomings. For instance, water can transmit trachoma and gonorrhea, ear, nose, and throat infections. Swimmers with heart problems can drown. Swimming does have two special points: first, you can swim for a long period, and second, the activity builds endurance. A good swimmer stores up *ch'i*. If he stores up *ch'i* for a long time he will have increased energy. By increasing endurance he can store up even more *ch'i*. Storing up *ch'i* for a long time will improve his breathing capacity and strength. If one can swim vigorously and increase his strength, he will become buoyant. Both of swimming's special points originate from its suppleness. Lao-tzu said "The way to concentrate the *ch'i* is to develop suppleness." T'ai Chi Ch'uan is different from other exercises because of this. Swimming can develop some aspects of this but not as well as T'ai Chi Ch'uan. From the standpoint of increasing strength and having no defects, T'ai Chi Ch'uan is superior to swimming. T'ai Chi Ch'uan's other name is *Ch'ang Ch'uan* (Long Boxing) because it is like a long river or ocean rolling on unceasingly. This describes the inherent continuity which is the concentration of *ch'i* and the embodiment of suppleness.

There is no difference between this and the function of swimming. Fish are the best swimmers. They were born and reared in the water, but do they know the role of the water? Humans are the best walkers. They were born and raised in the air, but they do not know the role of the air. One thing they share: If fish are plucked from the water, they will die; and if man is displaced from the air, he will also die. Water and air are different, but the need for them is the same. Man and fish are different, but if you change their positions the result will be the same; that is, man must have air as fish must have water. Therefore, my idea of swimming on land is appropriate. Man on land is swimming in the air, but he has long forgotten about it. No doubt you don't know the role of air. Great Air contains everything. The role of air is to imbue everything and sustain all materiality. People know the results but not the mechanism. The teachings of Huang Ti and Lao-tzu explain this clearly, but people hardly bother to study them.

One person may not be able to hold onto a chicken, while another can lift a large cauldron. People are the same, but why are their strengths different? Strength is based on *ch'i*. Some people are strong because their *ch'i* is strong. Their *ch'i* is strong because it has accumulated. The accumulation of *ch'i* is like that of water. If water is shallow, its floating power is weak; even a cup or a plate cannot float on it. If water is deep, then even a large ship can float on it and it doesn't seem heavy. It is because the accumulation of *ch'i* is deep that a person has strength and can lift up a heavy cauldron. If a person knows how to accumulate the *ch'i* as deep water is accumulated, then his force is unlimited and lifting up the heavy cauldron becomes easy.

The discussion of the storage of *ch'i* refers to accumulation in the *tan t'ien*. The *tan t'ien* is the *ch'i hai* (sea of *ch'i*) and is located 1.3 inches below the navel. It is named "sea" because of its large capacity and deep floating power. If the *ch'i* can travel to the "sea" and accumulate day by day, then in three years there will be significant enhancement. But this is siphoning only a little *ch'i* from the universe, as if one were to take only a single hair from ten thousand oxen.

How does one start to accumulate such *ch'i*? The answer is to learn the movements of T'ai Chi Ch'uan. By accumulating and mobilizing the *ch'i* through T'ai Chi Ch'uan, we fill the blood vessels and membranes down to the marrow, and this fullness radiates into the skin and the hair. Such is the concentration of *ch'i* to become supple. Swimming is the only other exercise that conforms to the principles of T'ai Chi Ch'uan and which concentrates the *ch'i* to become supple. The results depend quantitatively on the effort and time you devote to it, but day by day your progress will increase and there will be no limit. For this reason I use swimming as an example of T'ai Chi Ch'uan; the practitioner can immediately see the comparison. It is easy to comprehend that air, like water, is not empty. When you execute each movement, you feel your motion as if you were swimming. Closing and opening, floating and sinking, moving forward and moving backward—all are like swimming. If you can reach this level it is a great achievement.

How does a beginner start to practice this? You must wave the arm and let the palm move against the wind, feeling the air as if it were water. As you make greater progress the air will not only feel heavier than water, it will feel like iron.

Long ago my friend Mr. Ts'ao told me that scientists had made a new discovery. In experiments where air is forced into an iron receptacle and compressed under pressure, it becomes metallic. By using this receptacle as a bomb, the experimenters generated an explosion greater than a conventional weapon. I doubted this until the later invention of the atomic bomb. Then the idea that air is heavier than iron was no longer strange to me. T'ai Chi Ch'uan's movements are based on the accumulation of *ch'i*. Therefore, its power is stronger than the floating power of water. This is the lesson of the concentration of *ch'i* to become supple, which can overcome the hard. So I conclude that the idea of swimming on land is elucidative.

Treatise Six
Equal Importance of the Heart and Spine

The *Classic of Internal Medicine* mentions the *jen* and *tu* meridians together. Other books designate the heart and spine together. The Taoist literature clearly discusses the relationship between the heart and spine in the process of self-cultivation. T'ai Chi Ch'uan is an internal school of the martial arts. At the end of the Sung Dynasty, the Taoist Chang San-feng expounded the theories of action and non-action of the Yellow Emperor and Lao-tzu and combined them with the concepts *li, ch'i,* and *hsiang* from the *Chou Book of Changes* to create T'ai Chi Ch'uan. Basically these theories did not go beyond the *jen* and *tu* meridians. The *jen* and *tu* are the first of the extra meridians. The *jen* is governed by the heart and the *tu* is governed by the spine. Furthermore, the spine is connected with the kidney. If we differentiated them into substance and function, the spine is the substance and the heart is the function. Combined, the heart and kidneys behave as a unity. Because of this, T'ai Chi Ch'uan is better than any other martial art or other forms of exercise.

The heart is the ruler of the body. The essence of

the Chinese Philosophers tells us, "Seek the release of the heart-mind." Ch'an Buddhists ask, "Is the host at home?" Here the host is the heart. This is similar to the Taoist concept of the heart and kidney as connected together. Although their paths are different, they all arrive at the same place. T'ai Chi Ch'uan goes beyond this. It is said: "The best way is to understand by clear demonstration." Therefore, I have written this book in an attempt to show the truth that the substance includes application. Here the "heart" does not mean merely the organ itself. It refers to the mind. The heart and the mind are not two separate entities nor are they just one. The function of the heart as organ is wiser because of the inherence in it of the mind.

The spine has twenty-four vertebrae. In humans it is the major bone structure and is divided into sections. The internal organs are all affixed to it and at the same time it supports the torso. However, the structure of the spine is not as important as its function which is the path and means of self-cultivation and preserving life. T'ai Chi Ch'uan's basis lies also in this.

When the beginner starts to learn T'ai Chi Ch'uan, he should secure his mind and *ch'i* in the *tan t'ien*. Do not forget this, but also do not coerce it. This is the meaning of "seek the release of the mind" and "is the host at home." After a long time, the *ch'i* naturally passes through the coccyx, spreads along the backbone, and travels up through the occipital region to the top of the head. Then it descends to the *tan t'ien*. This is the unification of the *jen* and *tu* meridians and the coupling of the heart and kidney. You cannot, however, attain this after practicing just a short while. More importantly, you cannot force it! It must be completely natural. If you do attain it, your T'ai Chi Ch'uan desire has the potential to reach the highest level where your spirit will become immortal. Longevity and good health will be your lot.

It is difficult to describe the mind. People of knowledge and self-cultivation have foraged through the work of the ancient sages, their theories of secret transmission and of upright and unwavering mind like the passing of the sun and the moon through the Heaven. Concerning this I need not explain further. But I would like to expound more upon the word "spine." Generally, ancient people referred to self-cultivation as *cheng ching wei tso* (straightening the clothes and sitting upright). The derivation of the word *wei* is difficult. Most people do not dare to interpret it directly as meaning "dangerous." But I think the two words *wei tso* contain the actual meaning of danger because the spine, like a string of pearls, has many sections ascending vertically. If we ignore it even slightly, it will lean, bend, or collapse—and thus have no power to support the body. In cases of minor illness this will lead to abscess or consumption of the bone. More serious illness will cause the bone actually to break. Is this not dangerous? One who is adept at self-cultivation knows this and does not let flagging energy result in illness. Therefore, the words of precaution are: *cheng ching wei tso*. If you are *cheng* (upright), there will be no cause for illness in the spine. *Wei* is the fear of not being upright and so courting illness. So I advise T'ai Chi Ch'uan practitioners, "Make your spine upright." Upright is a string of pearls that does not lean. But being tense, holding oneself unnaturally erect, or overcorrecting are all real defects. You just have to know that these are dangerous. That is enough.

Treatise Seven

Strength and Physics

The use of *ch'i* and *chin* in T'ai Chi Ch'uan depends on their being continuously circulated unrestricted (throughout the body).

Within the universe there are objects large as the revolving planets and small as the perpetually falling droplets of rain and dew upon the earth. The natural shape of these objects is spherical. From their spherical shape we can infer various things about their substance, function, and also their composition which are in many ways similar to T'ai Chi Ch'uan. I will now try to illustrate this.

A planet is huge in dimension, and because of its spherical shape it revolves and is supported in space by *ch'i*. If its shape were not spherical, even the *ch'i* of the universe, which can support everything, could not support it and the many other planets so that they would float and revolve in space. Because of its intrinsic nature, the sphere is the shape with the greatest holding capacity (volume) for its surface area. Consequently, a single drop of rain or dew, although small, contains a maximum number of molecules, each one trying to disperse. While its surface thus has an expanding force, its inside has a contracting force—which results in an equilibrium. The equilibrium between these two forces minimizes the surface area; this is the reason why a sphere becomes a sphere.[1]

When the sphere is spoken of in connection with T'ai Chi Ch'uan it simulates the T'ai Chi symbol, since the way we use it to think about substance and application is similar to how we use it to reflect natural phenomena. Here I use a drawing to illustrate my meaning.

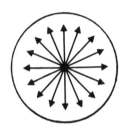 All points on the circle are equidistant from the center. Mo-tzu said the same, "*I chung t'ung ch'ang* (Within the same circle the radii are all the same length)." On the surface of a sphere there is the same balance of forces at all points; otherwise the spherical shape is quickly lost. It doesn't matter whether the sphere is made of iron or rubber. Regardless of what weight difference exists between them, if a force is applied to the sphere at a single point, the whole sphere must move in order for the sphere to remain spherical.

Because the body is like a sphere, T'ai Chi Ch'uan practitioners do not allow others to touch or feel them. By the same token, the opponent will be ignorant of where to direct his force. When the sphere is rotated, the molecules interact with each other by centrifugal and centripetal force, as is illustrated in the following drawings. The attraction from the center going out is centrifugal and the attraction at the surface of rotation going toward the center is centripetal. These two attrac-

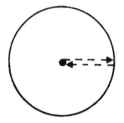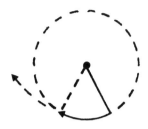

tions must be equal or the rotation cannot be maintained. For example, if you attached a heavy object to a piece of string and whirled it around, your hand would become the center and the turning object would be impelled by force to go outward. This force is named the centrifugal one. The force on the string that pulls the weight inward is the centripetal one. At this moment, even if the string is soft and pliable, the tension along it is strong. The relative strength or weakness carried through the string depends solely on the speed of the turning weight.[2] This is like the push-hands of T'ai Chi Ch'uan and may be referred to as the "pulling-the-saw style." If I should receive a strong centripetal force, then I would return an equal amount of centrifugal force. Even if I receive a strong centripetal force I can neutralize it as long as I can use the function of the principle of the sphere. When I return the centrifugal force, my opponent cannot neutralize it and he will be repelled a great distance. This so far describes only centrifugal and centripetal forces — an aspect of the functional use of the spherical force.

Within a circle there can be placed an infinite number of squares and triangles (polygons). The triangle is the basic underlying shape in the formation of a circle as can be seen in the following illustrations. The functional use of the circle is a consequence of the triangles which the circle contains. The applied physical use of the circle as described in physics is simulated in a cone or a screw.

  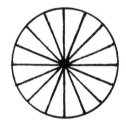

From these, it can be seen that rounded things are strong and not easily destroyed by outside forces in a negative defense. At the same time each circle contains many triangles that can then be used in positive offensive positions (attacks). If circular objects rotate, producing a forward and backward motion, then every part of the circle has a potential offensive function.[3] If, for example, the opponent spins the ball to you in table tennis and you do not respond appropriately you will lose. The success of this attack is because of the short distance between opponents and great speed of the many triangles contained within a circle. T'ai Chi Ch'uan uses a circle embodying this same kind of triangular motion and the result is obvious. It imitates the circle, not really the sphere. In defense we follow the circle, and in offense we use the triangle. In attack, every point on the circle is an angle of a triangle which rotates toward the opponent, and the opponent will find it difficult to escape. Therefore, in attack, it is possible to transcend the function of the circle and to convert it to an isosceles triangle, with even broader applicability, although still within the scope of the sphere.⁴ The following illustrations make this clear.

 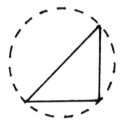

From these diagrams we can see that any action in T'ai Chi Ch'uan is an attack and every point is a defense. This is what we mean when we say that yielding is an attack and an attack is also yielding; the negative contains the positive. "The opponent doesn't know me, I only know him. From this approach one becomes a peerless boxer." The previous discussion concerns the offensive potential of the circle containing many triangles. There are times, however, when a force comes from the front causing one side of the triangle to collapse. What then would be the result? It is illustrated in the following diagram. As shown here when the force comes di-

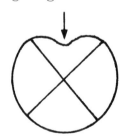 rectly from the front and without deviating to the sides or up or down, we no longer talk about turning left or right or cycling up or down as the way to yield. We talk only about receiving the attack. In T'ai Chi Ch'uan, we *use* the opponent's strong attack against him—which is what the *Book of Changes* describes as *K'an*, the trigram of "the Abyss" and the

hexagram of danger. This is the primary reason to use the term *"T'ai Chi"* to name this martial art, for it means to cause the attacking force to dissolve in emptiness. When the opponent realizes that he has failed, his only option is to withdraw and try to escape. During the opponent's withdrawal of his attacking force, my abdomen, which has absorbed and stored the force of his attack, uses this power to attack his retreat. This response is what the *Classics* refer to as *t'i-fang. Fang* means to release. I then become a circle again. The opponent will be at a loss as to what he can do and is thrown out a great distance. This *fa-chin* (releasing strength) is a unique characteristic of T'ai Chi Ch'uan.

The opposite of *fa chin* is [turning], *tsou* or *hua. Tsou* is to turn rapidly, and *hua* is to turn slowly. The turning in either case is the same. This is illustrated in the following diagrams. Neutralize the point of attack

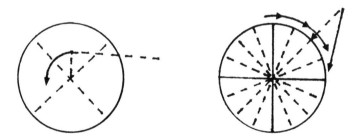

and the attacking force will naturally disappear. Simultaneously as you neutralize the opponent's force, the numerous triangles will turn and the angles of the triangle will become the offense. This is how neutralization becomes counterattack. *Tsou* is counterattacking and counterattacking is discharging. How can you use strength to attack and discharge? Follow the diagrams as models.

When you *fa chin* (release the internal strength) it is necessary to locate a straight line through the center of your opponent's body. The principle is similar to the sphere in physics. When you push on the sphere, your force must be delivered toward the center and in a straight line. The sphere will then have no opportunity

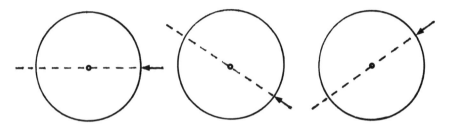

to turn. The opponent will fly straight out like an arrow or bullet. This is the principle of *fa chin* in T'ai Chi Ch'uan. If you desire your opponent to go up, across, or down, the straight line is the basic requirement. As long as you follow this rule, whatever you desire you will attain. My teacher, Professor Yang, always told me, "To *fa chin* you must always first find the straight line; then you can release the energy. When you release it, it is like releasing the arrow." There can be no better words to describe *fa chin*. It may be easy to understand the concept of the straight; however, when you try to apply it without comprehension and experience, you cannot get the results you desire. The practitioner must work hard. If someone asks, "Suppose I already understand the above principles and I am attacked by an opponent who is as strong as a bull, as fierce as a tiger or ram, and as ravenous as a wolf? What shall I do when he attacks as fast as lightning and thunder and has no regard for himself?" I would answer, "This is an important question. What I have explained above is precisely the technique to control such opponents. They are easier than hesitant opponents. The technique is completely described above." Here I will reiterate the principles.

The volume of a sphere is greater than that of any similar object of the same surface area. Even if someone attacks quickly he cannot transcend the conditions governed by space and time.[5] Since he cannot control these two paramenters then it is what-we-call "putting meat on the rack." He will get the contrary of what he desires and will be only more quickly defeated. Why? It is similar to a spent arrow that cannot pierce a piece of Shantung silk. This is a direct consequence of the limitation of space and a prolonged time period. The force is dissipated by the space it travels through and the time spent in its passage. The sphere comes to occupy more surface area and space. When space and time are increased, the change makes the speed ineffective and causes the function of the attack to disappear. This is the main goal of T'ai Chi Ch'uan. There is no defense; there is only yielding. There is no direct conflict; I merely evade him. Let his speed and power decrease; follow his tendency; then, attack. There is no need for excessive force. Let him promptly destroy himself. This is what the *Classics* mean when they refer to this as, "A force of four ounces deflects a thousand pounds." This is one level of proof. I will go on.

How can an arrow released from a hundred paces pierce seven layers of the target? First, you draw the bow with great initial force, then you release it. This is the impelling force. The arrow accelerates producing a force equal to or greater than the original force. For example, if the impelling force is one hundred pounds, the velocity can accelerate to a force of two hundred pounds. We achieve an impelling force of two hundred pounds by applying the relation: Force times Speed equals Energy. In physics we have the formula: Force × Speed × Time = Energy.[6] In T'ai Chi Ch'uan, "A force of four ounces deflects a thousand pounds" means that four ounces of strength can be the motivating force to dislodge a thousand pounds. Force times Speed times Time equals Energy. The opponent's energy is controlled and put to use by me and his force and speed become spent. Therefore, one can see that rapaciousness and ferocity are useless. The power of T'ai Chi Ch'uan is like that of a thin piece of paper, and the opponent's attacking force is like the crashing waves of a long river. How can you defend against it? If you defend against it frontally, nothing can stop it. But a piece of paper following the direction of the current cannot be destroyed. Paper is very weak. Yet if a piece of paper is placed on a rotating engine and spun up to two to three thousand revolutions per minute, the moment the paper flies off the spinning axle, it can slice a piece of wood in two. It is the same in T'ai Chi Ch'uan, where great strength comes from no strength. People should not neglect this fact. The function of our art is to excite the *ch'i* in the *tan t'ien* like the water in the Yangtze River. The *ch'i* magnifies the spherical movements of the body. Although the original strength is small, its speed is increased, and the result

surprising and immeasurable.

In the previous illustration, besides the offensive function of the isosceles triangle and the uses of the sphere (turning up and down or left and right), there is also the underlying use of the principle of the lever. The fulcrum is critical in the development of leverage. It provides the equilibrium in T'ai Chi Ch'uan in a fashion similar to what I have diagrammed. In the drawing, all the other parts of the lever, aside from the fulcrum, can turn in any direction. If you strike the right side of the lever, the left side will swing back. The space travelled in the rotation of the right side is greater and thus the time it takes to travel the distance is longer. This effectively reduces the opponent's attacking force to zero. If the right side of the lever receives one thousand pounds of force, the impetus will be completely transferred to the left side. The lever's right side swings back rapidly and the force of the lever's left side rotates forward. We have borrowed the opponent's force to counterattack. He will then be at a total loss as to what he can do and he will be repulsed a great distance. This is an example of T'ai Chi Ch'uan's *fa chin*.

In addition to this, T'ai Chi Ch'uan is useful in dissipating an opponent's strength and unifying one's own strength. Note the following illustration. When the opponent uses two hands to push me frontally by con-

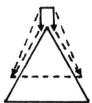 

tacting my forearms, I unite my two arms to form a wedge, splitting the strength of his forward push so that its force is reduced to zero. At the same time my wedge becomes an offense. I borrow my opponent's force to counterattack his vital areas. The *Classics* say, "Attract to emptiness and discharge." This is another method.

T'ai Chi Ch'uan is also excellent in its application of *t'i chin* (uprooting strength). Uprooting can cause an opponent's feet to leave the ground, resulting in his fall. The *Classics* say, "By alternating the force of pulling and pushing, the root is severed and the object is quickly toppled without a doubt." The application of leverage is similar to that of a jack or crane. It is like the following diagram. If the distance between the point of applied

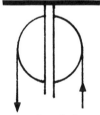 force and the fulcrum is longer, then we need to use less force to obtain a greater result efficiently. When we use *t'i chin* and *fa chin*, the opponent becomes the center of gravity, our hands and wrists touching the opponent become the fulcrum, and our foot and leg become the point of applied force. This is why in T'ai Chi Ch'uan

the *fa chin* or point of force is in the foot. The *Classics* say, "The motion should be rooted in the feet, released through the legs, controlled by the waist, and manifested through the fingers." Even if the opponent is big and strong, his size and strength is useless. When touched he will be repelled a great distance. All this depends on the application of leverage. Although we use the hands to make contact, the motivating force originates in the feet. This is wonderful and without equal! With half the work, the result is double. When you reach the highest level, the ratio of work to result cannot be measured.[7]

All of the above shows how the use of strength in T'ai Chi Ch'uan follows the example of natural phenomena in a way that is consistent with physics. T'ai Chi Ch'uan originates as philosophy, but, like science, it validates its principles empirically. The principles of T'ai Chi Ch'uan traditionally have been difficult to understand, and people had many doubts and reservations. Here we use the theories of physics to explain the application of strength in T'ai Chi Ch'uan. Even if T'ai Chi Ch'uan is based on philosophy we can examine it firsthand. But translating theories of physics and natural function and motion into T'ai Chi Ch'uan requires profound and difficult research. T'ai Chi Ch'uan must first have substance, then application, but without application, the underlying substance is useless. If you desire both substance and application, you must study the theory deeply. Then you can understand the wonderful uses of strength. This treatise reveals the secret of many generations of T'ai Chi Ch'uan masters. I hope the practitioner will pay attention to this!

Editor's Notes

1. The normal physical explanation for why a drop of rain is spherical is that the individual water molecules bounce off each other because of their energy of motion (expanding force), but they also have slight attractions to each other; in the interior of the drop, any given molecule is attracted equally on any side, so the attractions cancel out, providing a net expanding force; but at the surface of the drop, there is no attracting force from the outside of the drop, so there is a net attracting force directed toward the interior. If the drop were not round, then the forces on the surface molecules would be uneven in directions tangent to the surface, thus moving the molecules along the surface until the drop became round.

2. Notice that in his discussion of centrifugal and centripetal forces, Man-Ching is ignoring forces that are tangent to the surface of the sphere. Thus, he makes the distinction between inner- and outer-directed forces, but not between left- and right-directed forces.

3. To see the utility of round objects in negative defense, consider the roundness of the egg, "Nature's most perfect shape." Eggs are very difficult to break, since they either tend to roll away, or, because they are round, they can easily re-direct forces away from their centers along their surfaces.

4. The discussion about triangles can be more easily understood if the triangle is considered as an abstraction of the lever. From his discussion it appears that any one corner of the triangle can be considered to be the fulcrum of the lever, and that any force directed along one leg of the triangle (one end of the lever) will be re-directed back through the fulcrum to the other leg, and ultimately back to the originator of the force. This will neutralize the original force by directing it away from its original direction, along the surface of the circle (or sphere). This can happen as long as the triangle maintains its structural integrity, and the fulcrum of the lever

(i.e., center of the circle) remains fixed. Notice that the circle's center, or lever's fulcrum, need not be within one's own body; the important thing is that none of the legs of the triangle (or ends of the lever) collapse; that is, the spatial relationships between the forces do not change.

5. The limitations of time and space, and the desirability of the sphere make sense if you consider that the more space there is around you, the harder it is for anyone to transmit their attack. Since attacks may come from any quarter, it is best to be alert and keep one's distance equally from any direction.

6. An object moving at a constant velocity being subjected to a force over a period of time requires a certain amount of work. In the discussion of Force, Speed, and Energy, modern physics would actually say that Force $\times$ Speed = Power, not Energy. For example, a small force acting very fast, or a large force acting slowly, could both exert a lot of power, that is, the ability to deliver lots of energy quickly. Since Force $\times$ Distance = Energy, and Speed = Distance / Time, then Force $\times$ Speed $\times$ Time = Energy. Notice that a small force acting quickly can equal a slower acting larger force.

7. Rather than "weight point" and "point of force," it might be clearer to say "application force" and "balancing force," respectively. Though he makes the analogy of a jack or crane, it sounds more like a balance scale.

Treatise Eight

Maintaining Life and the Original State

Sometimes a single word can electrify a whole nation. The right man at the right time can accomplish miracles. The well-being of a nation rests upon the talents of its people. Mencius said, "A nation's talented people assume the burden of responsibility for their country. How hard they must work!"

But what will happen if talent is not supported by adequate physical condition? Sometimes a young person of great talent shows remarkable promise as long as he retains the early vigor of youth. But as time goes on, his condition declines; and before he is sixty years old (the time of reaching high office), he may do harm to others because of the dullness of age.

I think it is still easy to find talented people, but it is difficult to find truly cultivated ones. Yen Hui (one of Confucius' best students) died prematurely. K'ung Ming also died young. What can be a greater loss to the country than the untimely death of its most promising citizens? We all admit that this is a great pity, but what caused these deaths? Yen Hui's food basket and gourd were often empty, and K'ung Ming continued to work hard although he ate very little. Malnutrition and over-work are the reasons they died early. Mencius, however, was different. He said, "I am good at cultivating the Great *Ch'i*." Here Mencius surpassed the others. There-fore the lives of Yen Hui and K'ung Ming were shorter because they didn't cultivate the Great *Ch'i* like Mencius.

The chief technique in T'ai Chi Ch'uan is to culti-vate the *ch'i* and sink it to the *tan t'ien*. The *Classics* state, "The *ch'i* is always nurtured without harm." This saying is based on the words of Mencius. Today people want to emulate Mencius, but they do not know how to cultivate the *ch'i* or to practice T'ai Chi Ch'uan. They are not able to emulate him. If those who learn T'ai Chi Ch'uan do not know what Mencius meant by "Seek the released mind," they will find that their cultivation of *ch'i* is meaningless and simply tiresome. The *Classics* say that the mind and *ch'i* stay together in the *tan t'ien*. This is the "seeking of the released mind" to arrive at the perfect place of cultivation without harm. Do not force it and do not forget it. Let the Great *Ch'i* be naturally cultivated. When people practice in this manner, then they can establish their merit, their virtue, and their words. Do not worry about other matters. The way is simple and easy. Do not waste time. You know what air can be breathed and what air cannot. You can cultivate the *ch'i* while walking, sitting, standing, lying down, speaking, laughing, drinking, or eating. You can culti-vate the *ch'i* at every opportunity, inseparable from daily life. Consider these examples: While walking or sitting in a boat or car, or meeting relatives and friends, or listen-ing to music, or playing games, we can make use of these occasions to sink the mind and the *ch'i* to the *tan t'ien*.

If the air is fresh in the morning or evening, breathe more. When there is foul air, hold your breath and avoid inhaling it. When walking or sitting, standing or lying down, cultivate the *ch'i* in the same way. While walking, pay attention to the separation of the substantial and insubstantial foot. The center of the substantial foot should stick to the ground, and the arm that swings back should be substantial. The *ch'i* is manifested in the fingers. While sitting, you should always be *wei tso* with upright spine. While standing, one foot should be substantial with the center of the foot sticking to the ground. When you tire, change to the other leg. While lying down on your right side, bend your right leg and place the top of your left foot against the back of your right knee. The left palm rests on the left hip and the right hand braces the right cheek. Sink and relax your whole body so that it sticks to the bed. While talking and laughing, don't be too loud; the *ch'i* comes from the *tan t'ien*. When there is saliva it should be swallowed. Eat your meals at regular intervals and limit the amount of food. When eating, don't eat too fast and don't talk or laugh. Sink the *ch'i* and *wei tso*, and hold the bowl close to your mouth. Use the time to cultivate the *ch'i* and "seek the released mind." If you can do this, you can practice T'ai Chi Ch'uan at any moment all day long. This is my insight after twenty years of practice. The merits cannot be described in words. Then you need not worry about the "food basket and gourd being empty" nor about "working hard and having little to eat." The *ch'i* comes first in culitvating life. However, it is useless to talk to those who cannot or will not persevere.

Treatise Nine

Benefiting the Internal Organs

There are two kinds of martial-arts school: the internal and the external; that is, *Wu-tang* and *Shaolin*. *Wu-tang* is Chang San-feng's internal school of T'ai Chi Ch'uan. A Chinese proverb says "Internal schools train the *ch'i* and the external schools train the ligaments, bones, and skin." This means that the internal school expressly emphasizes the *ch'i*. To cultivate the *ch'i* it is necessary to sink the *ch'i* to the *tan t'ien*. When the *ch'i* sinks to the *tan t'ien* then it becomes strong. When the *ch'i* is strong, then the blood is full. When the *ch'i* is strong and the blood is full, then the internal organs benefit. Why? Because the internal organs of human beings are different from those of animals.

The animal's spine is horizontal like a beam, but the animal cannot stand upright like a human being. Therefore, the animal's internal organs hang from the spine in proper order. When the animal jumps, all the organs shake back and forth. This makes the connective tissues of the organs strong, and therefore, the animal's internal organs become healthier than those of humans. Human beings can stand up; their spine is upright. They are intelligent and wiser than animals, but their strength has declined. Why? Because the upright spine causes the internal organs to sag on top of one another and, thus, their surfaces stick together. Wet heat is produced and the resulting steam injures the spleen and stomach first. Then the lungs, intestines, and other internal organs deteriorate. People do not know why this is. They still think that the feet are adequate for walking and that walking alone can make you healthy. But it is not so. The legs are good for walking and exercise is better than being lazy. But, if you walk too much, you will hurt your ligaments. Although the internal organs shake when people walk, the organs still stick together and cannot rub loosely against one another in beneficial contact. Then the connective tissues of the organs are not exercised, and day after day undoubtedly become weaker. Only if you sink the *ch'i* to the *tan t'ien* will the result of exercise be different. The *tan t'ien* is located in the middle of the abdomen, 1.3 inches below the navel. The internal organs are above the *tan t'ien*, and when the *ch'i* sinks to the *tan t'ien* the internal organs can relax and move, and open and close, with each breath. This process is further helped by special exercises, such as the turning of the waist, the activation of the arms, the depressing of the chest, and the taking of steps, all of which will make the internal organs rub lightly against each other. These will not only strengthen the main connective tissues of the organs but will also dissipate the wet heat so that it cannot cause illness. Moreover, you will develop marvelous energy and be benefited in other ways. Sinking the *ch'i* to the *tan t'ien* can give each internal organ its own exercise. This is how T'ai Chi Ch'uan serves the internal organs. Do not seek the external, seek the internal, the *ch'i*. That is, the heart of the matter.

Treatise Ten

Recovery From Lung Disease

When I was young, I was weak and sickly. At twenty years of age I taught at Yu Wen University and also at a fine arts university in Peking. Then I taught at Chi Nan University and at an art academy in Shanghai. Before ten years had passed I had contracted tuberculosis from inhaling too much chalk dust. I later founded the College of Literature and Art of China in Shanghai. The blackboards were made of thick coarse glass with a green felt backing; a wet towel was used to erase them. After wiping, the blackboard could immediately be reused. This blackboard was utilized by my colleagues and students so they could avoid the lung diseases that I had contracted.

From the Sino-Japanese War till the end of World War II, the nourishment of school children was poor and many contracted tuberculosis. I felt great sympathy for them. Because they lacked nourishment and also inhaled chalk dust, they contracted tuberculosis. I hope that educators will heed this. As for myself, after I had practiced T'ai Chi Ch'uan for several months, my tuberculosis was cured. This, however, is my personal experience and is not sufficient to prove that T'ai Chi Ch'uan helps tuberculosis. My teacher, Yang Cheng-fu, and my classmate Huang Ching-hua taught T'ai Chi Ch'uan to tuberculosis patients and many recovered. Here I will describe briefly the pathology and treatment of tuberculosis.

In the medical *Classics* the lungs are called "a delicate organ." "Delicate" means fine and weak. Although we know the lungs are fine and weak, why do we not fear lung diseases as Western doctors do? Because the lungs are located above the other organs, they are called *hua kai*, or coverture, and are separated from the intestines and stomach. Western medicine cannot directly reach them and has no effective cure for lung diseases (besides surgery and the like). Chinese medicine is mainly based on transformation of *ch'i*. You must use the cultivation of *ch'i* for tuberculosis, or it cannot be cured. Therefore, it is easier to cure tuberculosis with Chinese traditional medicine than with Western methods.

There has been a fantastic improvement in the past three hundred years of Western medicine; but Western research is only from the external to the internal, based on the material aspects of the body, and assisted by high technology. Western medicine knows nothing about the transformation of *ch'i*. Therefore, Chinese medicine and Western medicine cannot help each other, which is lamentable.

There is no specific remedy for tuberculosis. If anyone claims to have one, it is a hoax. Why? The lungs directly contract only 3–4 percent of their pathologies. Besides the lungs themselves, there are the four solid organs and six hollow organs which can be the cause of lung disease. Wind, cold, dampness, dryness, heat, the seven emotions, and the six desires can all injure the lungs. How can you use a single kind of medicine to cure these different illnesses? For instance, the lungs may be ill because of stomach disease. If you heal the lungs and not the organic root of the disease, the condition in the lungs will recur. All the other organs can cause lung disease in the same fashion. This is but one example of interaction. In fact, all the organs have a mutually generating and mutually destroying function. If the principles of this function of complementarity are not followed, it will be impossible to cure diseases. Generating and destroying is the underlying transformative process of *ch'i*.

If you contract tuberculosis, it is necessary to resist it with the spirit and be brave so that the disease will not progress. For example, Chin Kuo-fu had the disease for many years, but he appeared to be normal. If someone is fearful and you tell him that he has tuberculosis, even though the disease is light it will become worse. Someone said to me, "If I had an X-ray and was told that I had tuberculosis, I would immediately collapse and not be able to get up." What can be done for such a person? Once in my hometown, there were two patients who visited a doctor. After the examination the doctor told the nurse to give medicine to the two patients. She was supposed to tell A that he had tuberculosis and to take care of himself, and B that he had caught a cold and would be fine after he took the medicine. The nurse, however, made a mistake by giving the wrong medicine to each of the patients and by telling each person he had what the other had. About two months later the doctor met A in the street and found him in good spirits and asked him how he had recovered. A said, "The nurse told me I just caught a cold and after I took the medicine, I recovered." The doctor was shocked but didn't say anything. By the time he returned home and sent someone to inquire about the other patient, B had already passed away. The doctor in the story is a friend of my classmate Ma Meng-jung. The doctor remarked, "The function of the mind is indeed strange!" This story was related to me in 1928 by Mr. Ma. In the winter of 1930 Liu Shen-chan asked me to treat his brother-in-law, Ch'eng, who had had tuberculosis for two years and was in serious condition. Ch'eng was the only son of the wealthiest family in Chu Ch'ao county. He had already visited many Western and Chinese doctors. Liu told him, "My teacher is a great doctor and it is not easy to see him. I sincerely begged him on your behalf to promise to treat you, so go quickly to Shanghai and be treated." He came to me and after I examined him, I purposefully did not tell him the truth. I said, "People believe you have tuberculosis, but they are wrong. You cough up blood because you have too much heat. After three doses of medicine you will stop coughing blood. When the bleeding stops, take care and in ten days you will be fine." Just as I recommended, he stayed in Shanghai for twenty days and then went home. After a year I went to Chu Ch'ao to see him. He was already much stronger. This discussion only deals with tuberculosis in connection with the spirit and bravery; it is not a description of the disease and its treatment.

Aside from the matter of spirit and bravery, if you directly tell patients that they have tuberculosis, it doesn't heal them but actually hastens their death. Pa-

tients who are told they have tuberculosis are then immediately asked to lie down and rest; however, their
mind is not able to rest. Even if they lie down and rest,
their mind becomes depressed. This is worse than death
because they suffer more. The more the body is at ease,
the more the mind works. The more the mind works,
the more the fire blazes up and burns the lungs. This is
what Chinese medicine calls the heart fire (the mind and
the heart are considered related organs in Chinese medicine). The lungs correspond to the element of metal, and
fire can melt metal. This is the heart-mind destroying
the lungs; in a short time it will burn everywhere. Western medicine does not know about this condition, so its
doctors tell their patients that this is either the first, second, or third term of their disease. It is just giving them
an invitation to a quicker death.

Tuberculosis patients should not always lie down.
Western doctors regularly encourage their patients to lie
down and this is a mistake. In ancient times people referred to the lungs as a hanging bell. When a bell hanging properly is struck, its clear ringing sound can be
heard from a great distance. However if the bell is laid
on the ground and struck, its sound is muffled and loses
its function. If you tell a tuberculosis patient to lie down
and not move, then, when he breathes, the lungs cannot
completely open and close and they progressively deteriorate. Concurrently, his digestive power becomes weaker
and even good nourishment will not help. When the patient always lies down this weakens the *Tu* meridian.
The *Tu* meridian is concordant with the spine and the
spine is the main support of the body. When the diges-

tion is weakened, the spleen will be weak. When the function of the *Tu* meridian is weakened, the kidneys are injured. When both the spleen and the kidneys are damaged, how can any patient be helped? This is beyond my knowledge.

How effective and reliable are X-rays? To my mind, they are not completely believable. People cough because their lungs have mucous, wetness, an obstruction, or congestion. There are some people who have had X-rays taken and were diagnosed as having tuberculosis; however, I was often able to cure them. Sometimes there are obstructions in the lungs which are due to the *ch'i* swelling the tissues and these could be misdiagnosed in an X-ray. When Wu K'ai-hsi was Minister of Foreign Affairs, the head of the Personnel Department was Cheng Chen-yu, one of my oldest friends. He had borne a pain in his left chest for more than ten years and he asked me to treat him. I diagnosed it as a swelling of the *ch'i*. Because he had had this condition for such a long time, it would have required one whole month to cure it. He thought, however, that taking one month to cure the condition was too long, so he wouldn't let himself be treated. In 1943, when Cheng went to the U.S. to work, he became ill. At a hospital in Washington, D.C. he had three X-rays taken and his condition was diagnosed as tuberculosis. The area was one-inch in diameter. A famous American doctor prescribed surgery. During the operation Cheng was cut open from under the armpit to the waist and from the back across one-half his abdomen. In the end the doctors were not able to find anything. He almost died and required many blood transfusions and was in bed for six months. Chen-yu has many friends who can confirm this. If X-rays are unreliable, then how reliable can stethoscopes be?

In the first term of tuberculosis the *ch'i* and blood of the patients have not been injured. At this stage the doctor must be brave and attack the condition in order to uproot the disease. If he treats it correctly, he can predict the date of recovery. Doctors no longer take into consideration whether the patient is hot or cold, excess or deficient, or suffering from wind evil, dryness or wetness. They just give him cod liver oil, concentrations of *Fritillariae* and *Semen Armeniacae Amarae*, and vitamins. These block the root of the disease in the lungs and prevent it from ever being cured. Such a treatment is called, "Cultivating a carbuncle" and "closing the door to kill the thief." It wastes time and is lamentable. I hope that the afflicted will ponder my words.

Tuberculosis is not incurable—I know this from experience. Some people eat a lot of garlic, turnips, millet congee, and loquats instead of rice and recover. Some drink *yang yu* (kerosene) and recover. In this way you are attacking the disease rather than supplementing it. If the patient spits up blood due to heat in the lungs, eating six raw eggs every morning may bring recovery within two months. There are also some who ingest *Portulacae* herb congee and recover, and there are some who have had tuberculosis for many years and recovered after eating several decoctions of human placenta stuffed in duck and cooked overnight. Some eat boars' lungs whose bronchial tubes have been filled with the liquid of twelve raw eggs. This is then steamed; after four or five doses they recover.

In the past twenty years I have cured many tuberculosis patients. The most serious were in the third term, and the doctors could no longer treat them. In Sung Chiang, I prescribed for Li Po-t'ing large doses of cinnamomi, aconiti, ginseng, and astragulus. After the first dose I knew I was right. After the second dose the disease was lighter. After eight doses he completely recovered. Later, Po-t'ing taught English at Huang P'o Military Academy. That was more than twenty years ago and his health is still good. In 1932, his six-year-old son had a fever and stayed in Central Hospital for six months. The diagnosis was congenital tuberculosis. By coincidence I was travelling from Shanghai to Nanking and treated him with a variety of cold herbs: antelope horn, rhinoceros horn, *Rehmanniae*, and *Ophiopogonis*. A few days later his fever was gone and he recovered. Now, strong and healthy, he is studying in the university. There are many such cases. I tell tuberculosis patients that the disease is not incurable, that they must not fret and worry or be afraid. If they can keep these three rules and take their medicine, they will see good results. It is especially important not to lose one's temper and become angry. Empathizing with their condition, I have researched many ways to cure the disease. I do not tire of the details and have compiled this information to benefit those who are ill.

I have stated that there is no special medicine for tuberculosis, however, T'ai Chi Ch'uan has a special advantage in treating this condition. People who hear this may think that it is only an advertisement to swindle them, but let me caution that T'ai Chi Ch'uan is effective only for those who can eat and walk and not for those who can no longer move. It is especially therapeutic in all lung diseases and without deleterious side effects. Let me explain:

T'ai Chi Ch'uan exercise first mobilizes, then leads to movement. One uses the *hsin* (mind) to mobilize the *ch'i* and then uses *ch'i* to move the body. This movement extends from the inside outward to the external. It originates in the internal organs and then is conveyed outward through the movements of the arms and legs. This is the process of sinking the *ch'i* to the *tan t'ien*, as previously explained. In short, one becomes supple through being light and agile. One must not use even the slightest force. Cultivate the *ch'i* and circulate the blood. Stretch your ligaments and conserve your energy. When you practice T'ai Chi Ch'uan in the morning or evening you only need seven minutes. It is especially important not to seek progress too soon.

Kidney energy deficiency is the cause of sixty to seventy percent of the cases of tuberculosis. In men this is a result of either excessive masturbation or wet dreams in their youth or over-indulgence in sex as adults. In women it is mainly from irregular menstruation or emotional upsets. During 1940–41 I was the consultant for the medical column of the *Citizen Commercial News*. Several thousand readers described their symptoms and asked for a prescription for tuberculosis. From this experience I have the evidence to confirm my medical theory. The kidneys are the sons of the lungs. The saliva from the lungs is transfered to the kidneys. When the kidneys are deficient in saliva, the semen dries up and the lungs will also be harmed. Because the lungs are injured they cannot supply sufficient saliva to the kidneys, and because the kidneys are dry the kidney fire blazes up, scorching and dessicating the lungs. This causes them to wither and develop chronic disease. It is also said that the lungs are like the branches of a tree and the kidneys are like its trunk. When the trunk decays, the leaves dry first and fall. The lungs are the weakest organ and will no doubt become diseased before the kidneys. The sinking of the *ch'i* to the *tan t'ien* in T'ai Chi Ch'uan is the function of the fire under water as in the Hexagram "After Completion." This is the only way to strengthen the kidneys. If the kidney *ch'i* is strong the lung *ch'i* will recover. This is a special result of T'ai Chi Ch'uan, and no one can dispute it.

Spleen deficiency can also cause lung disease. When the spleen is weak there is no appetite and poor digestion. The spleen is the mother of the lungs, and therefore the *ch'i* of the lungs depends upon the spleen. If the stomach contains food, the spleen will help to digest it. After the food is digested, the *ch'i* will be strong. The spleen is the first organ to receive the *ch'i*; it transports *ch'i* to the lungs. Consequently, the spleen is considered the mother of the lungs. For example, when you are hungry, the first organs to feel weak are the spleen and the stomach. Then starvation affects the lungs. The voice has no sound and the spirit withers. This shows that the lungs have lost their support. Sinking the *ch'i* to the *tan t'ien* accumulates *ch'i* in the abdomen. If you do not have food you can survive only for forty-nine days. I saw this in the instance of Mr. Su. It has been said that most people cannot survive longer than seven days without food. I once stayed with P'u Chi-p'ing in Nanking. I tried not to eat for eight days. I talked, I laughed, and I moved as usual; I lost only a little weight. This is one demonstration that the *ch'i* can provide for the spleen. When the *ch'i* sinks to the *tan t'ien*, the spleen becomes strong and the stomach has a greater capacity for food and better digestion. This no doubt vitalizes the lungs and is a special result of T'ai Chi Ch'uan.

When tuberculosis becomes a chronic disease the continuous coughing causes the lungs to lose considerable *ch'i*. The saliva becomes dry and wet heat predominates, causing the lungs to wither and become chronically diseased. Spitting up blood is not as serious as the chronic illness of the lungs. Clearly if the lungs are diseased there can be no *ch'i* inside. However, if you sink the *ch'i* to the *tan t'ien*, you can accumulate it and fill the lungs. If this is assisted by very supple, very slow, very light, subtle movements, gradually the lungs will open and close and reverse their deterioration. If the lungs are not weakened, then vital energy continues to flow and the old is regularly pushed aside to give birth to the new. If the lungs are kept from withering, even a decayed spot in them can be cured through nourishment and medicine. They will gradually return to health. T'ai Chi Ch'uan activates their ability to cleanse themselves and develop new tissue. This is its everlasting effect. There is much more I'd like to say on this, but—forgive me—there simply isn't space.

Treatise Eleven

The Levels of
T'ai Chi Ch'uan

There are three different levels of T'ai Chi
Ch'uan — Heaven, Earth, and Human. The
Human Level relaxes your sinews and vitalizes your blood; Earth Level "opens the gates" so that
the *ch'i* can reach the joints; and Heaven Level exercises
the sensory function. Each level has three degrees. The
First Degree of the Human Level relaxes your tendons
from the shoulders to the fingers. The Second Degree
relaxes your tendons from the hip joint to the "bubbling
well" [point in the bottom of each foot]. The Third
Degree relaxes your tendons from the sacrum to the top
of the head (*ni wan*). The Earth Level First Degree
sinks the *ch'i* to the *tan t'ien*. The Second Degree moves
the *ch'i* into the bubbling well. The Third Degree circulates the *ch'i* so that it reaches the top of the head.
The Heaven Level First Degree is *t'ing chin*. The Second
Degree is *tung chin*. The Third Degree is omnipotence.
These are the three levels and nine degrees.

Human Level

1. "The technique of relaxing the ligaments from

the shoulder to the wrist." If the ligaments can relax, the blood will circulate better. The sequence is first to relax the wrist, then the elbows and shoulders. Do not use any force. From softness alone will you gradually progress. All is based on seeking the straight from the curve. The shape is round — neither bent or straight. It is without breaks or holes, hollows or projections. Essentially you relax your ligaments to the tip of your middle finger. This is the Human Level First Degree.

2. **"From the hip joint to the heel."** The technique is as above, the difference being in the separation of light and heavy, of insubstantial and substantial. The foot must take the weight of the whole body and is different from the hand which can move unimpeded. Most people do not pay attention to the substantiality or insubstantiality of the feet. Even some martial artists ignore this basic issue. But T'ai Chi Ch'uan practitioners must place their weight on one foot and change from one foot to the other without using force. From the hip joint through the knee to the heel — all three parts need to relax. The weight rests on the center of the foot, which is supported by the ground. The feet must be separated into *hsu* (insubstantial) and *shih* (substantial) as must the arms. However, there is an opposition between the arms and feet. If the right foot is substantial then the left arm is substantial and vice versa (this is refered to as "cross-substantiality"). If the left foot is insubstantial, then the right arm is insubstantial. Imperfect separation of substantial and insubstantial is called "double weight." This is Human Level Second Degree.

3. **"From the sacrum to the headtop."** The technique is

as above. The spine with its many vertebrae is the major bone of the body. It is referred to as "the soft waist which can be folded up a hundred times as if it had no bones." From this description it is obvious that the spine must be pliable. The spine is pliable because of the ligaments. The most important point is to keep the sacrum upright and the head suspended as if from a silk thread. This is the Human Level Third Degree.

Earth Level

1. "Sinking *ch'i* to the *tan t'ien*." This is the cornerstone of cultivating the *ch'i*. The *tan t'ien* is located in the abdomen 1.3 inches below the navel, closer to the navel than to the spine. The requisite principle of sinking the *ch'i* is that the breathing must be fine, long, quiet, and slow. Gradually inhale into the *tan t'ien*. The *ch'i* stays with the mind, and, day after day and month after month, it accumulates. This must happen naturally and not be forced. In the beginning, it is not easy to lower the *ch'i*. You must sink the shoulders and elbows slightly, thus drawing the *ch'i* into the stomach. Relax the chest downward and slightly raise the back; then you can lead the *ch'i* to the *tan t'ien*. This is the Earth Level First Degree. If you don't practice in this manner, then you will inhale too quickly and the *ch'i* will go up. This will cause the shoulders to shrug and the chest to expand, and will readily lead to problems.

2. "**The *ch'i* reaches the arms and legs.**" After the *ch'i* sinks to the *tan t'ien*, it is commanded by the mind and led to the hip joint, then to the heel. This process is referred to as "the true man breathing down to the

heels." The *ch'i* next reaches the shoulders, elbows, and wrists. All the joints of the four limbs become open. Then the *ch'i* can go down to the "bubbling well" point on the bottom of the foot and up to *lao kung* in the palm of the hand, extending to the tip of the middle finger. Then you can experience what the *Classics* refer to as "the mind mobilizes the *ch'i* and the *ch'i* mobilizes the body." This is Earth Level Second Degree.

    3. **"The *ch'i* moves through the sacrum (*wei lu*) to the top of the head (*ni wan*)."** This refers to the *ch'i* going through the "three gates." It is the beginning of the connection of the *Jen* and *Tu* meridians. Getting the *ch'i* to go through the sacrum is the most difficult part. After a lengthy period of sinking the *ch'i* to the *tan t'ien*, you will reach a certain level where the *ch'i* will automatically go through the coccyx. You must not force it or the effort will be in vain and will cause problems. Be careful! You must follow the guidance of a teacher and fellow students. When the *ch'i* goes through the coccyx, it penetrates and pushes up between the shoulders into the occipital area and then to the *ni wan*. All of this occurs in the same way—first entering the door and then gradually approaching the Tao. Longevity and good health will be the natural reward. This is the Earth Level Third Degree.

Heaven Level

    1. **"*T'ing Chin*, Listening to or Feeling Strength."** What is *Chin* and how can we listen to it? This is a question which the practitioner must carefully study. *Chin* is different from *li* (strength). The secret transmis-

sion says, "*Chin* comes from the ligaments and *li* comes from the bones." This is a profound truth; yet today's students are blind to it. They will practice until they die and still never know what *chin* is. For them you can only sigh! *Chin* is *chin* because it comes from pliable veins which have a springlike force. It is only through pliability that you can stick to your opponent. When you stick to him, then your *ch'i* and his *ch'i* make contact. Through this contact of *ch'i* you begin to anticipate his attempts. This is called *t'ing*. The *Classics* say "If he moves a little I move first" on which *t'ing* is based. This is Heaven Level First Degree.

2. "**Comprehension of *Chin*.**" There are different levels of *tung chin* and *t'ing chin*: deep and shallow, fine and rough. If my opponent moves even slightly, I can hear and comprehend him. When I comprehend his *chin*, then I can move first. Having the correct timing and position depends on me and not on him. This progression is from the shallow to the deep. But the dichotomy of fine and rough is more difficult to explain. The secret transmission says, "If my opponent moves slightly I can hear and understand him." Even his slightest movements are still easy to discern. If you can hear others before they move then you have reached the level of enlightenment. What happens at this level is merely this: the *ch'i* goes through the ligaments, the vessels, the membranes, and the diaphragm, generating, respectively, four kinds of *chin*: defensive, concealing, ready to attack, and attacking. The joints can extend and contract because of the ligaments. The blood circulates because of the blood vessels. The membranes lie between the mus-

cles and gird the ligaments and bones. The internal organs are all bathed in it. The diaphragm is above the liver. If the opponent's *ch'i* originates from the ligaments and is normal, then it means he is defensive. If his *ch'i* is in the vessels, then you know he is concealing it and it will change. If his *ch'i* is in the membranes and surges up to the surface, it means he is ready to attack. If his *ch'i* is in the diaphragm, he is gathering the *ch'i* and preparing to attack. At this highest level of *tung chin* (comprehending strength), nothing can be more wonderful. This is Heaven Level Second Degree.

3. **"Omnipotence Level."** This stage of enlightenment is difficult to describe. The end of the *Classics* say, "Throughout the body, the *i* (mind) relies on the *ching shen* (spirit), not on the *ch'i* (breath). If it relied on the *ch'i*, it would become stagnant. If there is *ch'i*, there is no *li* (external strength). If there is no *ch'i*, there is pure steel." These words are very strange. They imply that the *ch'i* is not important, and in fact, it is not. When the *ch'i* reaches the highest level and becomes mental energy, it is called spiritual power or "the power without physical force." Wherever the eyes concentrate, the spirit reaches and the *ch'i* follows. The *ch'i* can mobilize the body, but you need not will the *ch'i* in order to move it. The spirit can carry the *ch'i* with it. This spiritual power is called "divine speed." In physics, speed is multiplied by force. The potentiation is unlimited. Therefore, spiritual power becomes "divine speed."

Students give up the immediate to seek the exotic; they don't understand the sheer marvelous function of the *ch'i* accumulating in the *tan t'ien*. The *ch'i* is just like wind, water, and clouds. They each can store up power as the universe itself stores up the primal *ch'i*. Mencius talked about cultivating the "Great *Ch'i*,"which is omnipotent and indestructible and fills up the entire universe. It is easy to observe and comprehend the power of wind and water but not that of the clouds and *ch'i*. Not until the advent of the airplane did we begin to realize that in black clouds there is thunder and lightning, that anything the lightning touches will be unavoidably shattered. Therefore, the accumulation of *ch'i* can support the universe and is beyond speculation or discussion. Spiritual power and "divine speed" are replicated [microcosmically] in thunder and lightning. This is referred to as the omnipotent level and is Heaven Level Third Degree.

This is then the order of progress in learning T'ai Chi Ch'uan. If students follow the sequence and do not skip ahead, then they can reach the highest level. I understand the aims of Chang San-feng and Wang Tsung-yueh and I continue to strive for their goal of making our race and country healthy and strong. I think this is the best path and I hope all students exert themselves in this direction.

Treatise Twelve

Comprehending Creation and Destruction

The Thirteen Postures are the "eight gates" and "five steps" and they correspond to the eight trigrams and Five Elements. *P'eng* (Wardoff), *Lu* (Rollback), *Chi* (Press), *An* (Push), *Ts'ai* (Pull), *Lieh* (Split), *Chou* (Elbow), *K'ao* (Shoulder) correspond to the hexagrams *Ch'ien, K'un, K'an, Li, Sun, Chen, Ken, Tui.* Step forward, step back, look left, look right, and central equilibrium correspond, respectively, to metal, wood, water, fire, and earth. Creating and destroying is based on the theory of complementary creation and destruction [in the *Book of Changes*], and is confirmed by the substance and function of the martial arts. Metal in the martial arts corresponds to the saber; wood, to the staff; water, to the sword; fire, to the spear; and earth, to the form. All things come from the earth. This means the saber, the staff, the sword, and the spear all come from the form. The use of the saber is an effect of hardness; it is adroit at chopping. If the staff meets the saber, the staff will be splintered. Metal overcomes wood. The disposal of the staff is reaching; it is good for thrusting. The form is empty-handed. When it meets the staff, it will be injured. Wood overcomes earth. The form is a technique with stability. When the sword encounters its stability, the sword will be controlled by it like the bare hand grasping the sword. The applicability of the sword is based on softness. When the spear encounters the sword, the spear will lose its ferocity. This is water overcoming fire. The efficacy of the spear lies in its ferocity; it is good for piercing. When the saber encounters the spear, the saber will lose its hardness. This is fire overcoming metal. All these are martial-arts terms which have been transmitted over a long period of time. They mean what they depict.

Weapons, however, only show how they overcome each other. The "five steps" contain the theory of both production and overcoming. For example, "step forward" has the nature of ferocity and corresponds to fire. Central equilibrium has the power of stability and corresponds to earth. When one steps forward with stability, there is no confusion and it is easy to prevail. This is fire producing earth. "Looking left" has the nature of hardness and corresponds to metal. It refers to stepping to the left while the right fist follows with stability. This is earth producing metal. "Step back" uses the quality of suppleness and corresponds to water. "Looking left" is hardness and supports the suppleness. This is metal producing water. "Looking right" has the essence of strength and corresponds to wood. "Stepping back" is suppleness, but it does not extend to the ultimate of softness. Therefore, it must be connected to strength. This is water producing wood. "Step forward" corresponds to fire and it has a fierce nature. With wood supporting it, its function is expanded. This is wood producing fire. The whole sequence is referred to as the "five steps" and it contains the function of the mutual production of the Five Elements.

The cycle of mutual destruction is essentially water overcoming fire. Fire advances with fierceness, and water withdraws with softness. The hotter the fire the cooler the water. This corresponds to the cycle of complementary destruction in physics. The rest can be derived from my explanation of the sword and staff.

The eight trigrams are different. They must exist in the context of *yin* and *yang* and the Five Elements. The *Book of Changes* says, "Therefore, the eight trigrams succeed one another by turns, as the firm and the yielding displace each other." *Ch'ien*, heaven, is metal. *K'un*, earth, is the element of earth. *K'an* is water, and *Li* is fire. This is *P'eng, Lu, Chi, An*, and corresponds to the four cardinal directions. It is the principle of *yin* and *yang*, or hardness and softness. This is the basic technique of the Thirteen Postures. Although there are four movements, in reality there is only the application of the two movements of *yin* and *yang*. Within these two, Rollback is especially dangerous and decisive. The *Book of Changes* explains *K'an* as concavity; it heralds danger because it has steel on the inside and softness on the outside. Military strategy does not generally go beyond this. The military employs deception after deception and never tires of them. All this strategy, however, does not completely capitalize on the marvelous uses of *K'an* (or concavity) and the warning of danger. Likewise, the application of T'ai Chi Ch'uan is one movement: *Lu* (Rollback).

The trigram *Chen*, thunder, is wood. *Sun*, wind, is also wood. *Ken*, mountain, is earth. *Tui*, lake, is metal.

These techniques are *Ts'ai* (Pull), *Lieh* (Split), *Chou* (Elbow), and *K'ao* (Shoulder). The four corners and the four cardinal directions combine to form the Fu Hsi Former Heaven Arrangement. *Ts'ai* corresponds to *Chen*, thunder, and is *yang*. On the surface it has both *yin* and *yang* and gives the appearance of instability between substantial and insubstantial, but *Chen* is the element of wood and can also produce fire. The original meaning of Pull is to move slightly the opponent's root, the purpose of which is to test the substantial and insubstantial. If the opponent is really substantial, then I pull him. There is no one who will not fall down. If he absorbs it and shows some change, then I give up and also change. This is the process of the eight trigrams mutually succeeding one another. If the opponent uses my pull and counterattacks with his shoulder—and if at this time I really pull—I will no doubt fall backwards. But if my pull is not real and if my opponent counters with a shoulder, it will be in vain (empty) and (attacking emptiness) he will fall down. This is an example of hardness and softness mutually displacing each other, or the fire of *Chen*, wood, overcoming metal. *Lieh* corresponds to *Sun* which is wind and wood. *Chou* corresponds to *Ken*, or mountain and the element of earth. Wood overcomes earth in exactly the same application; therefore, I need not explain further. This is the Five Elements acting from their own *yin* and *yang*.

Yin and *yang*, *hsu* (insubstantial) and *shih* (substantial), mutually exchange and transform. This is still easy to understand, but its way of changing without change is more difficult to comprehend. Change and the changelessness is the first principle of the Thirteen Postures.

Change is the continuous exchange of *yin* and *yang*, hard and soft. The Thirteen Postures mutually affect and displace one another. Everything changes. The changeless is the principle of the Thirteen Postures which constitute the stabilizing power of the central equilibrium. What is this stabilizing power? "Central" means always in the middle, equally disposed. "Stabilizing" means not immobile but never losing equilibrium.

The changeless does not worry about what attacking posture the opponent takes. If the opponent uses Wardoff or Rollback, I know it is Wardoff or Rollback. If he is *yin* or *yang*, *hsu* or *shih*, I know it is *yin* or *yang*, *hsu*, or *shih*. I always respond with my central equilibrium. I am neither pulled nor do I pull. I don't discharge nor do I let others discharge me. This is the principle of changelessness. If you can keep this principle, you can pull or push as you like, mutually exchanging. The use of any combination of these is fine. This is called "walking on the edge of the knife." We can see the difficulty of practicing the central equilibrium if we do not keep to the principle of the Doctrine of the Mean.

So I say the unified substance and application of the Thirteen Postures is built upon the *application* of Rollback and the *substance* of central equilibrium. There is nothing more—a single *yin* and a single *yang*: the Tao. This is T'ai Chi Ch'uan and it is the final principle which cannot be changed. Therefore, I use this as the governing theory of the *Thirteen Treatises*. Is it not appropriate?

Treatise Thirteen

Explanation of the Oral Secrets With Forward and Commentary

In olden times when martial artists discovered a great technique they would not usually reveal it to others. The transmission would be by "handing down to the son and not the daughter." Not all sons were talented, however, and they often lost the technique. If the teacher had good disciples he would teach them the secrets but would withhold one secret for emergency situations. In such a climate, it is impossible to develop the martial arts.

I cannot say that what I learned from my teacher, Professor Yang, was all that he had to transmit. If I also keep one secret or if I keep all of them, I would then be guilty of saving a pearl while my country went to ruin. For more than ten years I have tried on many occasions to transcribe these secrets so that they could be spread widely, but each time I had this intention I stopped because I also was afraid of transmitting them to the wrong person. I thought it over many times. To share good things with others is my true heart's desire. Therefore, I carefully wrote down the following twelve secrets. These twelve were secrets that my teacher did not lightly pass down to anyone. Each time he spoke, he reiterated to me, "If I don't tell you, even in three life-times you will not easily get it." These words were ut-tered many times. I felt fortunate that my teacher loved me greatly but regret that I could not fulfill his expecta-tions. I hope that other talented people will study this and spread it so that all people can be healthy and have long lives. In this way the teaching will benefit the human race.

1. **Relax** (*sung*). My teacher must have repeated these words many times each day. "Relax! Relax! Relax completely! The whole body should completely relax!" Otherwise he said, "Not relaxed. Not relaxed. If you are not relaxed, then you are like a punching bag."

To comment on the single word *sung* is extremely difficult. If you can relax completely, then the rest is easy. Here I have written down what my teacher told me daily in order to make his teachings understandable to others. Relax means to soften the tendons and blood vessels of the whole body. You cannot permit even a lit-tle tension. This is known as "a soft waist that can fold a hundred times as if it had no bones." If you had no bones and only ligaments, the ligaments could then relax and open up.

2. **Sink** (*ch'en*). If someone can relax completely, then this is *ch'en*. If the ligaments and blood vessels relax, then the whole body (of which they are a part) sinks down.

Basically, *ch'en* and *sung* are the same thing. *Ch'en* means not floating. Floating violates T'ai Chi Ch'uan. If your body can sink, this is already good, but you must also make the *ch'i* sink. If the *ch'i* sinks, then the spirit (*shen*) gathers. That is very useful.

3. **Separate Insubstantial and Substantial.** The *Classics* say, "Every place has the same insubstantiality and substantiality." This is because the right arm and the left leg are one stream of strength. The right leg and left arm are also the same. If the right arm and left leg are substantial, then the right leg and left arm are insubstantial, and vice versa. This is called "clearly separating." In short, the whole body's weight rests on only one leg. If two legs equally carry it, this is double-weightedness. When the weight is transferred, the sacrum and the uppper back must be kept upright in the middle. Then you will not lose your equilibrium. This is very important.

The "transfer" of weight is the key to the change of insubstantial and substantial. If this is not explained, then you won't really know where to begin. The key point of the transfer of strength from the right hand to the left hand is in the upper back, and the key point in the transference of strength from the left leg to the right is in the sacrum. The sacrum and the upper back must be straight and upright. Then you will not lose equilibrium. You must carefully study these words, otherwise you will not comprehend them.

4. **"Raise the strength to the top of the head."** This means that the energy at the erect top of the head is light and agile. This is also called suspended headtop.

The process of "suspending the headtop" is similar to tying someone who has a queue to a beam so that his body hangs down in the air [above the ground]. He can rotate his whole body, but he can neither bend back nor drop his head, nor lean it to either side. This is the meaning of "suspend the strength to the top of the head" and "suspending the headtop." When you practice, the occipital bone should be upright. Then the *shen* and the *ch'i* reach the top of the head.

5. **"The millstone turns but the axle does not turn."** The turning of the millstone represents the turning of the waist. "The axle not turning" is equivalent to the equilibrium that comes from the sinking of the *ch'i* to the *tan t'ien*.

"The millstone turns but the axle does not turn" is really the transmission of the family secret. In light of what the *Classics* tell us ("the waist is like the axle" and " . . . the waist [is] the banner"), its meaning is obvious. Since I learned this I find improvement every day.

6. **"Grasp Sparrow's Tail is like two men sawing."** This is the push-hands sequence of Wardoff, Rollback, Press, and Push. The action is like that of sawing. When you saw, the force at both sides should be equal; then the action is smooth. If one side tries to change the force, the saw's teeth will bind. If my partner binds the saw, then even if I were to use force I would not be able to draw it back. Only if I push it will it saw smoothly as before. This has two meanings for the push-hands of T'ai Chi Ch'uan. The first is to give up oneself to follow others. In following the opponent's tendency you can learn the marvelous application of *hua chin* (neutralization) and *tsou chin* (yielding). Second, "If others move slightly, I move first." This refers to the situation wherein my opponent uses force to push me and I obviate his attack by pulling back first. If the opponent uses pull I preclude this by pushing first.

The principle in the example of pulling the saw

brings great clarity. Through it, I suddenly comprehended how to practice the idea, "if others move slightly, I move first." If I am familiar with this, then the push-hands is controlled by me and not by my opponents. The rest is obvious.

7. **"I'm not a meat rack; why do you hang on my body?"** T'ai Chi Ch'uan seeks relaxation and agility and to avoid stagnation. Stagnation is like dead meat hanging on a meat rack. How can you say it has spirit? You must criticize this practice severely. Therefore, we have these words [of admonishment]. This is also a secret family transmission. It has a very deep meaning that requires careful study.

8. **"Being like the upright [punching-bag] doll that cannot be pushed over."** The whole body is light and agile. The root is in the foot. If you have not become adept in relaxation and sinking, you cannot easily do this.

The center of weight of the upright doll is located in the lower part. The *Classics* say, "Sinking to one side is responsive; being double-weighted is sluggish." If both feet use force simultaneously or if the whole body is stiff and sluggish, one push can knock you down. Generally, the whole body's weight should sink one hundred percent onto one foot. The rest of the body is relaxed and light as a feather. If you can master this, you cannot be pushed down.

9. **"Being able to *fa chin* (discharge strength)."** *Chin* (strength) and *li* (force) are different. *Chin* comes from the ligaments and *li* comes from the bones. Therefore, *chin* is soft, lively, and flexible while *li* is hard, dead, and stiff.

What is *fa chin*? It is like shooting an arrow. Shooting an arrow depends on the spring force of the bow and string. The force of the bow and string is soft, lively, and flexible. *Chin* and *li* are different and the ability to discharge or not derives specifically from this difference. This, however, is discussing the quality of *fa chin* but not its function. Here I'll transmit the technique of *fa chin* which my teacher periodically described to me. It is said, "Seize the moment and opportunity." It is also said, "The feet, legs, and waist must act together simultaneously." Old Master Chien-hou liked to repeat these two verses, but "Seize the moment and opportunity" is the more difficult of the two to comprehend. I now perceive that the action of sawing contains both the "moment" and the "opportunity." When the opponent moves forward or back, I already know it. This is obtaining the "moment." The opponent's action of advancing and retreating while being controlled by me is obtaining the "opportunity." "The feet, legs, and waist must act together simultaneously" means the power is concentrated so that you can discharge your opponent farther. In the meantime the body will not move dividedly and you can "hit the target." This is the function of *fa chin*. Students should study it diligently.

10. **"In practicing the form the body should be level and upright, and the movements should be consistent."** This sentence is very easy to understand but difficult to practice. The upright body must be stable and comfortable to be able to absorb [force from the eight directions]. If the movements are consistent, then they are strung together and there is no place where they are

broken. The *Classics* say, "Stand like a balance" and "Mobilize the *chin* like pulling silk from a cocoon." Therefore, students must work hard in studying these principles.

11. **"Study conscientiously. The Song of Push Hands says, 'Be conscientious in *p'eng, lu, chi, an*'."** If you are not conscientious, then the push-hands won't be realistic. Now I'll tell you, if you Ward Off to your opponent's body or Rollback to your own body, both are wrong. If you don't Ward Off to your opponent's body and you don't Rollback to your own body, it is correct. *Chi* and *an* must store up the strength and not lose the equilibrium. This is correct.

I will comment on the phrase, "study conscientiously." Even after examining the *Classics* of T'ai Chi Ch'uan many times, I still did not understand them until I received my teacher's instruction. Then I realized it had a particular method. Without the guidance of oral instructions, it was impossible to understand. Parts of the *Classics* are like this. They truly require the secret family transmission. Students must inquire into this so that they will grasp the key points and not lose their equilibrium. This is crucial.

12. **"Use four ounces to deflect a thousand pounds."** People do not believe that four ounces can deflect a thousand pounds. It means that you can use four ounces to offset a thousand pounds, after which you apply Push. So leading and pushing are two different things. You are not really using four ounces to push a thousand pounds.

We must separate "offset" and "push." Then you

can explain their marvelous functions. For example, the water buffalo weighs a thousand pounds, but the rope through its nose is a mere four ounces. To use the four-ounce rope to offset the thousand pound buffalo is precisely the technique of leading. You can lead as you like, but the buffalo cannot do as it wishes because it is offset by its nose. If it were led by the horns or leg, it would not work. Therefore, to lead the opponent is a particular method. For a buffalo you can use a four-ounce rope to lead it. However, if it were a thousand-pound stone horse, could you do it? No. This is the difference between the living and the dead. Humans have spirit. When they use a thousand pounds to attack, they have a direction. If the attack is straight, I use four ounces to lead the end of his hand. I follow his tendency and shift to the diagonal direction. This is an example of leading. After his force dissipates, I push him. There will be no one who will not be thrown. Only four ounces of leading force are needed. The power of the push is then up to me. The power of the leading force should not be excessive or else the opponent will intuit it and be able to mobilize and escape. On occasion I can use the leading force to change his direction and attack him. If he detects my lead he will store up his force and not advance. When he stores up his force his tendency is to withdraw. Follow his withdrawal, give up the leading force, and discharge him. Then there will be no one who will not fall down. That is the countermove.

The above was my teacher's oral instruction and I do not dare keep it to myself. I wish to spread and share it with all T'ai Chi Ch'uan friends.

Afterword

Practitioners of T'ai Chi Ch'uan must first of all
understand the essential [meaning] of its substance and
application. To understand the application you must
work on the substance. The substance is the root while
the application is the branches. When the substance is
completed the application is already there. The comparison of T'ai Chi Ch'uan to self-cultivation and good
health goes without saying. In this book the chapter on
"Strength and Physics" is based on modern scientific
research and the other chapters are based on the T'ai
Chi Ch'uan principles. I still fear that those who study
T'ai Chi Ch'uan will not easily find the hidden door.
Therefore I have taken a few ideas from physiology to
confirm the following.

First, the *tan t'ien* in T'ai Chi Ch'uan is the only
path for the Taoist; there is no other way. The *tan t'ien*
lies in the abdomen close to the navel and goes back
toward the spine. It is located about 1.3 inches below
the navel. In physiology it is referred to as the center of
gravity of the body and is located in the middle of the
waistline. The center of gravity of the body is referred to
in T'ai Chi Ch'uan as *chung ting*. The *chung ting* cannot be separated from the *tan t'ien*. The *Classics* say,
"Pay attention to the waist at all times;" "controlled by
the waist;" and "the waist is like an axle." In other

words, T'ai Chi Ch'uan could also be called an exercise that emphasizes the center of gravity of the body. The *Classics* say, "Stand like a balance;" "The upright body must be stable and comfortable to be able to support (force from) the eight directions;" and "Don't lean in any direction." These words refer to seeking upright balance (alignment) and not losing the center of gravity.

Second, the most important process in T'ai Chi Ch'uan besides the *tan t'ien* is that "when the sacrum is straight, the *shen* (spirit) goes through the top of the head" and then you "suspend the strength to the top of the head." These two phrases are the key points. The first phrase describes the sacrum and the top of the head, and the second phrase refers to the flow through the *yu chen ku* or occipital region. The Taoists refer to these areas as the Three Gates—the sacrum, the occipital area, and the headtop. Physiology calls these parasympathetic nerves which of course are located in the same place as the Three Gates. The sympathetic nervous system is the spine, and its function is dissipation. The function of the parasympathetic nervous system is recovery. How can you recover through the parasympathetic nerves? You accomplish this through the diaphragm which naturally contracts, expanding the chest, and pressing down on the internal organs of the abdomen, which in turn stimulate the parasympathetic nerves. This cycle causes the breath and pulse to slow down and increases the flow of saliva. It decreases the blood sugar and lowers the blood pressure. It also facilitates the flow of urine and reduces fever. This is all a result of the *ch'i* sinking to the *tan t'ien* and the coccyx staying straight so that the *shen* goes through to the headtop. If you know these two principles then you can talk of self-cultivation.

Third, there is the issue of physiological changes. Fifty years ago the woman's world in China was confined to the family. Because she was restrained by social customs, men and women were not in close social contact. Word from the outside could enter her room, but her own words could not go out. Her feet were bound and her chest was tied down. These two practices injured the body.

Women in China today not only have unbound feet and chest, but they participate in many sports and work in society just like men. There is a big difference between former and modern times. The benefits for modern women are greater today, but they are not purely advantageous. For women, nuturing the blood is very important. The blood needs quietness in order to be nurtured, a process which is different from the cultivation of the *ch'i*. This quietness was traditionally developed through softness and patience, which, on the other hand, caused melancholia. This malaise made the blood cold and caused it to congeal, and thus led to illness. Modern women, on the other hand, abuse themselves and readily expend their blood like boiling water. This causes delayed or no menstruation and sometimes leads to consumption. The excess is just as bad as the deficiency. I believe that the strength or weakness of a nation or race depends upon the health of its women. If the women are healthy, then mothers will be strong and their sons will be strong. Otherwise, both will be weak. It is like planting a seed. If the soil is rich the crops will be plentiful;

if the soil is poor then the crops will be bad. Women need exercise but in moderation. No matter if we are young or old, we all desire a strong and healthy body. The best exercise is T'ai Chi Ch'uan. The most important qualities of T'ai Chi Ch'uan are suppleness, quietness, and lightness which are all beneficial for a woman's body. In that regard, it is better than any other exercise. I am a traditional Chinese doctor and I wrote this book to give people a choice. The wise will choose it.

Cheng Tzu's Thirteen Treatises on T'ai Chi Ch'uan

Section II

緒論三篇 Additional
Sections

Explanation of the Essential Points

T'ai Chi Ch'uan has traditionally consisted of about 120 movements, many of them repetitions. I have doubts about these repetitions, for they are of no benefit to the substance and application. I have come to believe there are three reasons for them. First, it was feared that the practitioner had no perseverence and, therefore, the time of the set was purposely prolonged in order to cultivate perseverence. Secondly, in the set there are some basic movements the student *must* repeat and practice if he is to improve. Thirdly, the (original) set of thirteen postures was too short and required too little expenditure of energy.

Of these three reasons, perhaps none of them is quite valid. It is difficult to cultivate perseverence in those who do not have it. It doesn't matter how long you practice; when you stop, it is always the same. Also, a teacher can select basic postures which require further practice, and let the students work on these independent of the connected form. If the set is too short then repeat it, but to repeat repetitive postures many times is meaningless and unnecessary.

On many occasions I tried to simplify the form but was too busy to complete the the work. Then, in 1937, the Sino-Japanese War occurred and I was put in charge of the Martial Arts Department of Hunan Province. It was my job to train all people in the martial arts. T'ai Chi Ch'uan was an important part of this curriculum. I had to simplify the form in order to spread it, and I had to spread it so that it could make the people and the country strong. As a result, my friends and T'ai Chi Ch'uan practitioners alike praised my work. I wrote this book because of the extraordinary times and circumstances and not to exhibit myself.

I hope my readers may offer their comments.

Professor Yang's Essential
Points of T'ai Chi Ch'uan

1. When Professor Yang taught students the form
or push-hands, he would say, "In practicing T'ai Chi
Ch'uan, don't move the hands by themselves. If you
move the hands, it is not T'ai Chi Ch'uan." To empha-
size this point he would cite authority: "When old
Master Chien-hou taught people, he always quoted the
Classics: 'The feet, legs, and waist must act together
simultaneously.'" He also quoted the line, "'It is rooted
in the feet, released through the legs, controlled by the
waist, and manifested through the fingers,'" which
likewise means that the hands must only follow and
must not move by themselves. From this, it can be seen
that the beginnings and the ends of movements cannot
be separated. Moreover, in the beginning of the *Exposi-
tion of Insights into the Practice of the Thirteen Postures*
it is said, "The *hsin* mobilizes the *ch'i*, the *ch'i* mobilizes
the body." This is also evidence that the hands must not
move independently. T'ai Chi Ch'uan is T'ai Chi Ch'uan
because the external and the internal become unified as
one. Any discussion of T'ai Chi Ch'uan not in accor-
dance with the above principles falls beyond my realm.

2. "Sink the shoulders, drop the elbows, and 'sit the
wrist.'" This means that the shoulders should neither be
shrugged nor collapsed. The elbows should not be raised
nor squeezed. If they behave naturally, they will auto-

matically sink. To "sit the wrist" is the most difficult of the three, as it requires that the veins and tendons do not appear on the back of the hand in order to be correct. This is traditionally called "beautiful lady's hand." The fingers are neither closed nor open, and neither bent nor straight. One seeks the opened from the closed and the straight from the curved. The *ch'i* must pass through the *lao kung* point (Pericardium 8) in the palm before it can reach the tips of the fingers.

3. "Sink the chest and pluck up the back." Sinking the chest means you should neither distend nor hollow the chest. You must relax it to be correct. To pluck up the back is difficult to explain.* It means that the *ch'i* circulates through the "three gates."

4. "Sink the *ch'i* to the *tan t'ien*." The *tan t'ien* is in the abdomen 1.3 inches below the navel (Jen 6). It is anterior toward the navel and posterior from the *ming men* (gate of life) located on the back.† To sink the *ch'i* is to will the *ch'i* to accumulate in the *tan t'ien*, but not to stuff the abdomen. Be careful!

5. "Effortlessly the *chin* reaches the top of the head." The head should not lean in any direction, neither forward nor backward, left nor right. It should be suspended by keeping the coccyx upright so that the *shen* (spirit) can reach the top of the head (*ni wan*).

6. Knees. In the beginning posture or when just standing naturally, do not lock the knees. In the postures

---

* The upper back rounds a little because of the hanging chest and pectorals.

† One-third of the distance to the spine.

such as "Brush Knee" or "Single Whip" the knee should not go beyond the dorsum [toes] of the foot. The instep should be soft as cotton and the "Bubbling Well" (Yung Ch'uan) relaxed and sunken into the ground.

These six points are so important that I selected and placed them in the beginning so that students would pay more attention to them.

The Respected Transmission

This book is the result of Professor Yang Cheng-fu who was my teacher and of his T'ai Chi Ch'uan book, *T'i Yung Ch'uan Shu*. This book completely follows my teacher's instructions and is a continuation of his book. Because the traditional form was too long, people lacking patience could not easily finish it and, therefore, did not continue practicing. I simplified the form by deleting the repetitions; this made it possible for the practitioner to go from the easy to the difficult. I called my work Simplified T'ai Chi Ch'uan. My classmate Professor Ch'en Wei-ming encouraged my work and urged me to publish it. I believe this book is in harmony with my teacher's ideas.

For three generations, the Yang family taught this T'ai Chi Ch'uan only to the Imperial Family of the Ch'ing Dynasty. Therefore, most people did not know about T'ai Chi Ch'uan until the beginning of the Republic of China. Then it gradually spread to Kiangsu and Chekiang Provinces. I had a lung disease and, for this reason, I started studying T'ai Chi Ch'uan. Because I studied for so long [under the guidance of a knowledgeable teacher] I received the true transmission. I would now like to share this tradition with others and, therefore, I have written down all its secrets. I not only desire my country to be strong, I would also like to share the benefits of T'ai Chi Ch'uan with all mankind.

The theories of the *Classics* of T'ai Chi Ch'uan are wonderful. Its principles can be applied not only to daily life but to military theory, as well. After studying for twenty years, I wrote down the main points, which became these *Thirteen Treatises*. I hope students will continue to practice even after they become healthy, for the path of self-cultivation and longevity also originates here. T'ai Chi Ch'uan is different from medicine, which only helps a specific part of the body; it doesn't have the shortcomings of meditation which, although it makes the *ch'i* labor, doesn't exercise the body. Ts'ai Chueh-ming [a famous Chinese educator at the turn of the century] said, "It is a self defense and it can make your body strong. In the use of this exercise, there are a hundred benefits without one harm. It is a model for the whole country to follow." His are words full of wisdom.

簡易太極拳秘要圖解

Important Secrets of
Simplified T'ai Chi Ch'uan
Diagrams and Illustrations

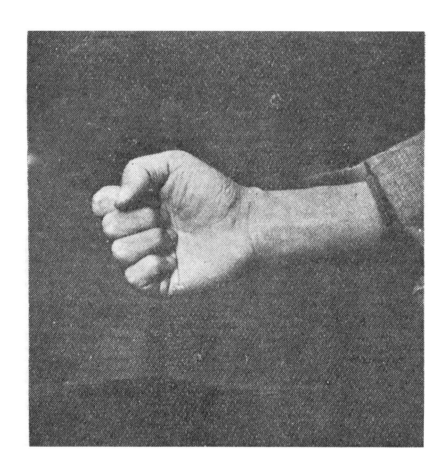

Fist

The fist is similar to an ordinary fist. The outside appears tight but actually is not. The inside is relaxed. The wrist should be straight and not bent.

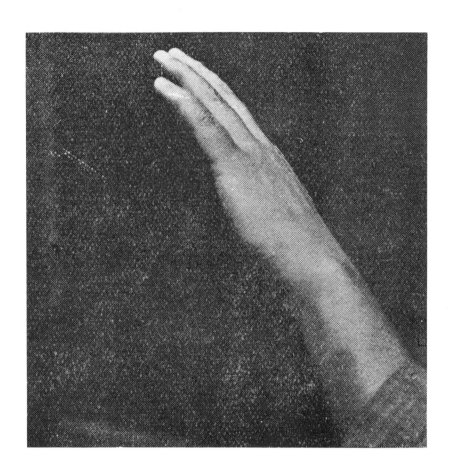

Open Hand

Traditionally, this is called the beautiful lady's hand. The blood vessels and tendons on the back of the hand should not stand out. In every posture, the wrist should be straight.

Single Movements

1. Preparation Posture

This is the preparation posture of T'ai Chi Ch'uan. It is also the standing posture used to cultivate the life principle. From a state of attention, first shift the weight to the right leg. Bend the leg slightly and sit on it. Lift the left leg and move it one step to the side. Then shift the weight to the left leg. Raise the right toe and turn it to the front, placing it straight ahead. The two feet are parallel and separated. The distance between the feet is shoulder width. At the same time the two elbows are slightly bent and the backs of the wrists are straight and face forward with the palms facing down. The fingers are raised and point slantingly forward, and are neither spread apart nor closed together. The head should be upright. The eyes look forward and the attention should be directed inward. The ear listens to the breath, and the tip of the tongue touches the front of the palate. Close the mouth. Sink the shoulders, drop the elbows, and depress the chest. This causes the *ch'i* to sink to the *tan t'ien*. The breathing should be long, fine, quiet, and slow. This posture represents T'ai Chi before it separates into *yin* and *yang*. Externally and internally, the whole body should be relaxed and completely natural. From the sacrum to the top of the head the *i* and *ch'i* should be connected. This is the "suspended top of the head." I remain quiet, waiting for the opponent's move; then the inner and outer become one. Thus, substance and application are completed. Most people neglect this posture. Who would have thought that the way to practice and

Posture 1

the applications are all based on this one? When you begin to study, you must be very clear about this.

2. The Beginning Posture

Beginning is the first posture. This is T'ai Chi giving birth to the *Liang I* (the Two Primordial Powers). *Liang I* is *yin* and *yang*. *Yin* is shape. It is below and therefore earth; it does not move. *Yang* is *ch'i*. It is above and is heaven. It is light and clear, and it floats. In the beginning use the *hsin* to mobilize the *ch'i*, and sink the *ch'i* to the *tan t'ien*. When the *ch'i* fills up internally, the two arms follow the *ch'i* and float up. This uses the *ch'i* to mobilize the body. The *ch'i* enters and the body inflates upward. When the arms drop, the situation is reversed: the body deflates and the *ch'i* goes out. After this, the *ch'i* is used to mobilize the body, and the actions of floating, sinking, inflating, and deflating are all based on this.

The main purpose of this movement is to begin opening and relaxing the wrists. The wrists change six times. From the attention posture to the preparation posture is one change. From the preparation posture to the beginning posture the arms rise up, like floating up in water. The backs of the wrist point upward, and the fingers point downward. This is the second change. When the wrists rise to shoulder height, the *ch'i* mobilizes to extend the fingers. The tendons and blood vessels are neither stretched nor loosened. This is the third change. When the arms move back, the wrists and elbows fold up in front of the shoulders, and the fingers point downward again. This is the fourth change. When

Posture 2

the arms go down, the wrists change as if they were sinking into water; the finger tips float on the water surface. This is the fifth change. Then the arms move to the sides of the hips as in the preparation posture. This is the sixth change. This is why I say the beginning posture emphasizes the exercise of the wrists.

Grasp The Sparrow's Tail (Third Through Seventh Postures)

Grasp the Sparrow's Tail is similar to an ancient dance called "Grasping the Oxtail," and it is the collective name of Wardoff, Rollback, Press, and Push. It is also the basis of T'ai Chi Ch'uan. In push-hands, *chan, lien, t'ieh, sui, pu tiu, pu ting* cycle without stopping. The arms as they interact with each other resemble a sparrow's tail.

3. Wardoff Left Side

From the beginning posture, if the opponent uses his right fist to strike my right chest, I immediately sit down on my left leg; my right chest follows my waist, turns to the right, and relaxes. At the same time, I pivot on my right foot (on the heel), raise my right hand horizontally to the level of the armpit, and touch the opponent's wrist with the palm facing down. The left hand lines up under the right hand with the palm up at the level of the right hip joint. My eyes look forward, prepared to take the offensive. At this moment the opponent knows his strike is in vain and withdraws his right fist. He will then strike with his left fist, but I have already sunk on my right leg, and my left hand wards off

Posture 3

his left arm. The left leg steps forward in a straight line, the knee bent, and I sit on it. I straighten the rear leg slightly. The left leg becomes substantial and the right leg becomes insubstantial. Both hips should be level and facing forward. The sacrum should be slightly inward so that the trunk is upright. At the same time, the left hand gradually wards off at chest level with the palm facing inward. The elbow is slightly dropped. Then my wrist lightly adheres to the opponent's forearm. Using a light touch to control his arm and wrist, I await his change. Simultaneously, the right hand drops to the right hip to maintain balance.

4. Wardoff Right Side

From the previous posture—if the opponent is on my right side, and uses his right fist and left leg simultaneously to attack my left chest and groin, then I immediately use my right hand to encompass the intervening space with my left hand with palms facing each other vertically. Relax the left shoulder and use the right arm to protect the groin. The opponent knows that his force is in vain, and he has to stop his attack. I quickly turn the right hip, turn the heel of the right foot in place to the left, and step forward about one inch while the right knee bends and I sit on it. The right elbow immediately wards off in front of the chest, with the palm facing inward. The left hand is placed between the right forearm and chest. The eyes look forward. Straighten the left leg a little, slightly turn the left toe, and follow the waist. Use the Wardoff power of the right elbow to meet the opponent. There will be no opponent who will not be thrown out a great distance.

Posture 4

5. Roll Back

From the previous posture—if the opponent neutralizes my Wardoff and begins to push me, I quickly relax, drop my right arm, and cycle up around the outside of his left elbow. Using the inside of my right elbow, I stick to the outside of his left elbow. Simultaneously, the back of my left wrist touches his left palm, and my left elbow sticks to his right palm. At the same time, I sink on the rear (left) leg, the waist cycling to the rear. The arms follow the waist, cycling to the left rear. His push is in vain, and he loses his balance. In this moment, I can *ch'ien, po, ts'ai,* or *chou;* it depends on me. "There is plenty of room, more than enough to play about."*

* Chuang-tzu, "Secret of Caring for Life."

Posture 5

6. Press

From the previous posture—if the opponent withdraws his arm, I turn my right wrist, using the outside of my right elbow to stick to the outside of his left arm. My left hand adheres with the palm sticking between my right elbow and wrist. As the opponent withdraws his arm, I straighten the left leg and shift forward onto the right leg. Following the waist—with eyes straight ahead—I press upward. Then the opponent must be uprooted.

Posture 6

7. Push

From the previous posture — if the opponent neutralizes my press and lifts his right arm to press me, I immediately turn the right hand over. The palm pushes his right wrist. I separate my left arm, and the left palm pushes his right elbow. First, use the *t'i chin* to draw back, then push horizontally forward. The waist and leg simultaneously follow the eyes forward. Then the opponent will fall.

Posture 7

8. Single Whip

If the opponent attacks from the left rear, I immediately shift my weight to my left leg. The right toe raises slightly and turns to the left. Both arms are extended forward with their elbows dropped slightly and their palms down. These follow the waist, turning to the left rear corner, and the right foot turns 120°. Then shift the weight to the right leg and sit on it. The arms follow and swing back. The right hand stops at the side of the right chest (by the armpit), as the five fingers join together and drop into the shape of a hook. The left hand follows the right, simultaneously, palm up, and stops under the lower ribs below the right hand and above the right hip. As you extend the right hook to the right corner, the left heel turns in, pivoting on the left toes, and the knee and hip follow the turn counterclockwise. The hooked right hand extends to the right corner at the same time. "Seek the straight in the curve." Then the left leg lifts and takes a step to the left front. Bend the leg and sit on it. The right leg also "seeks the straight in the curve." At the same time, the left palm faces inward. The chest is level and it follows the waist as it turns until the waist faces the rear. The right toe follows the cycle of the waist and the left palm immediately turns over, approaching the opponent's chest. "Sink the shoulders and elbows." "Seek the straight curve." The eyes look forward. There will be no opponents who will not be thrown out. This is also a *chan kung* and extended *ting chin*. The body opens out but the *ch'i* must have central equilibrium.

Posture 8

9. Lift Hands

If the opponent attacks me from the right side, then I quickly turn my body to the right and sink on my left leg. I lightly raise my right foot to the front of the right side with the heel just touching the ground. The toes are slightly raised and the knee is slightly bent. Both arms open at the same time with the palms facing inward. Slowly they come together and ascend, until the right palm and right leg face straight forward. The left palm is in front of the left ribs; the right hand is extended beyond the left. Both hands have the same shape; the back of the wrist is straight and slightly bent inwards. You are trying to touch the opponent's wrist. Store the energy and lift him up. Wait for his change. If you can raise the opponent's energy, you immediately release him. Then there is no opponent who will not fall down. This is also one of the *chan kung*. It is the *ting chin* of *t'i ho*. Therefore, the grasping, the releasing while stepping forward, the step back, the look to the left, the look to the right all depend on me not on the opponent.

Posture 9

10. Shoulder

If the opponent attacks again, I quickly withdraw both arms and the right leg; the power of the opponent's pounce is negated. Immediately take a step with the right foot; place it straight ahead, and shift forward on it. Drop the right hand to protect the groin. The left hand is placed at the right elbow, and the right shoulder follows the power of the legs and waist. Following the line of sight, shoulder forward. Then there is no opponent who will not fall down.

Posture 10

11. White Crane Spreads Wings

If the opponent attacks with his fist and foot from the left side, I immediately raise my right hand from the left front to my right forehead. This neutralizes the opponent's strike to my head with his right fist. To protect my groin, the left hand simultaneously drops and brushes the left side to block the opponent's right-foot kick. My left foot moves to the front with only the toes touching the ground. Then the opponent's attack is thwarted.

Posture 11

12. Brush Knee, Left

If the opponent, using fist or foot, attacks my left side, or my middle or lower body, I immediately sink. My weight still rests on the right leg. I turn the right palm upward. Following the waist, the right hand drops down. When the hand reaches the right hip, the left foot steps out with the heel touching the ground. Simultaneously, the left hand follows the right hand to the right hip. When it begins to brush the knee, the right arm cycles up from the rear to the ear with the fingers pointing forward as if they were poking the opponent's chest. Meanwhile the left hand moves, palm downward, to the left thigh, to block the opponent's fist or leg. I shift the weight to the left leg and sit on it. I relax the waist and hip joint. Sink the shoulders and drop the elbows. The right palm follows the eyes. When the right leg extends the palm goes forward. Then there is no opponent who will not be thrown out.

Posture 12

13. Play *P'i P'a* (Lute)

If the opponent uses his left hand to block my right palm and attacks the right side of my chest with his right fist, I immediately pick up my right foot. I then put it down, and shift my weight onto it, the toes turned out slightly. This way I store up power. The right palm withdraws along the inside of his right wrist and forces his wrist diagonally downward to the left. At the same time, the left hand raises and sticks to this right elbow. The arms come together, as if holding a lute. Then the opponent's elbow is in danger of being broken, and he is completely controlled by me. This is called playing the lute.

Brush Knee, Left

Repeat the twelfth posture as described above.

Posture 13

14. Step Forward, Deflect Downward, And Punch

If the opponent blocks my right palm with his left hand and attacks my chest with his right fist, I shift my weight back and sink on my rear leg. The right palm follows and drops to the left hip to protect my groin. If the opponent's attack has failed, I fear that he will kick my groin. When I know that his attack is in vain, I immediately turn out my left toes about three inches, shift my weight to my left leg, sinking on it. Simultaneously, I lift up my right foot and take a half step to the right front, then sink onto it. The right hand becomes a fist which follows the waist forward and cycles down from the left to the right side, stopping at the right hip to neutralize the opponent's straight punch. This is called *pan* (deflect). The left hand simultaneously follows the turn of the waist, and cycles upward to ear level. The left palm comes up and strikes forward, to prevent the opponent's second attack. This is called *lan* (parry). While the left palm strikes forward, the left leg simultaneously takes a step. As its heel touches the ground, I immediately shift the weight onto it. The right fist follows the waist and the energy from the right leg, then punches forward under the left palm and wrist. The opponent is suddenly surprised, and the punch "hits the mark every time." This fine technique is honed by practice and sharpened by comprehension.

Posture 14

15. Withdraw and Push

If the opponent uses his left hand to grasp my right elbow and his right hand to pull my right wrist, I immediately open my right fist and withdraw it to the left shoulder. I sink on the rear leg to neutralize his control. The left palm turns up and crosses under the right elbow. The left palm follows the elbow to protect the arm and break the opponent's grip on the wrist. Simultaneously, with palms facing inward the two arms cross and fold toward the chest, neutralizing the opponent's grasp. This is called *feng* (seal), as in sealing the door. At the same time, depress the chest and relax the waist and hips. The left hand sticks to his left wrist, then pulls it slightly. The right hand sticks to his left elbow. (Now both palms face forward). Push forward and sit on the left leg. This is called *pi* (closed), as in closing the door and not being able to open it. This technique converts a disadvantageous position to an advantageous one. It is easily done and always under my control. It is without peer.

Posture 15

16. Cross Hands

If the opponent strikes from above on my right side, then I quickly move the right arm up to the right corner. Following the waist and leg, I completely open to the right side and, at the same time turn in the left toes to support the power and throw opponents out on both sides. The left arm follows the waist and turns. If the opponent uses two fists to attack the chest, I withdraw the body and sink on the left leg. The two arms drop and come together, and I use my wrists to stick to the opponent's wrists. The arms cross in what-is-called *shih tzu shou*. At the same time, the right foot moves back and is placed straight as in *ch'i shih* (beginning posture). This posture opens completely, then closes again. This is a wonderful application of opening and closing. The feet are both flat, but the left is substantial and the right insubstantial. This is not the riding-horse posture, which is double weighted and prohibited in T'ai Chi Ch'uan. You must ignore this (the riding-horse posture).

Posture 16

17. Embrace Tiger, Return To Mountain

If the opponent attacks me at close range from the back of my right side, and I cannot tell whether he attacks with hands or legs, I turn the waist quickly and separate the hands, the right palm down and the left palm up. The left hand drops behind the left side to brush off the opponent. Pick up the right foot, and take a step to the right rear corner, and sink on it. The right hand brushes past the knee and the palm turns up. This is to protect the groin and at the same time embrace the opponent's waist. If I miss, then I turn the left palm and strike the opponent's face. If I miss again, the opponent will withdraw the right hand and attack with the left hand. Then I use the Rollback posture. After this, use the three postures of Grasp the Sparrow's Tail: "Rollback," "Press," "Push," and "Slanting Single Whip," which are described above. Generally, each exchange of push-hands must be followed by three techniques. The rest of the postures are like these, so prepare in advance. The purpose is always to win. "Slanting Single Whip" faces toward the left rear corner. For the explanation, refer to "Single Whip" above.

Posture 17

18. Look At Fist Under Elbow

If the opponent attacks from the left front with his fist, I sit back, thwarting his attack. Quickly lift the left leg and take a step to the left front, and sink your weight on it to take the offensive. At the same time, the left hand sweeps to the side to guide the opponent's arm. Open the hook hand, and turn the waist leftward to change the opponent's offense. At the same time, the right leg takes a step to the right front. The toes point diagonally right and are in line with the left heel. Shift the weight to the right leg and sink on it. The two arms, parallel to the ground, follow the turning waist to neutralize the opponent's attack. When the right hand is ahead of the chest and the left hand is behind the left shoulder, step with the left foot to the front, its heel touching the ground. This avoids the opponent's grasp. At the same time, the left wrist makes a small circle and the fingers poke forward from under the left armpit toward the opponent's throat. The right hand moves back to the chest and becomes a fist under the left elbow. If the opponent grasps my left hand, my right fist can punch his stomach. When you use this punch you will never miss. Anyone you hit in this way will go down. You must use this method very carefully.

Posture 18

19. Step Back to Repulse the Monkey: Right Side

If the opponent's right hand holds my left forearm, and his left hand holds my fist under the elbow, then I will be controlled by him and can do nothing. Immediately, open the right fist, its palm up, and withdraw it to the side of the right hip. Turn the wrist of the left hand to face forward and push down to neutralize his grasp. If this fails, quickly take a step straight back with your left foot and turn the left palm upward to neutralize his grasp; then withdraw it to the side of the left hip. The right palm circles back and turns up to the ear, its fingers pointing forward to poke the opponent's throat — or the palm may be used to strike his chest. At the same time, the right toes turn straight to support the power. This posture appears to withdraw but really advances; it seems like a defense but is really an offense. The secret is in the waist. Study this carefully. The feet move back on a straight track. Most people do not understand. T'ai Chi Ch'uan comes originally from Taoism. When you meditate and the *ch'i* cannot get through the Three Gates, you have to practice this posture more.* If the toes of both feet turn out, the gate of the *weilu* will be closed. This can be discussed only with people who already know it.

---

* Three Gates: *niwan, yuchen, weilu.* The *niwan* is located at the top of the head, the *yuchen* at the occipital region, and the *weilu* in the sacral area.

Posture 19

20. Step Back to Repulse the Monkey: Left Side
The explanation is given above.

Posture 20

21. Diagonal Flying Posture

If the opponent grasps my right fist from my right side, I immediately turn the wrist and move it to the left beside the left hip. At the same time, the left hand circles up with palm downward under the armpit in front of the left chest to protect the right arm. If the opponent gives up the wrist and grasps the left elbow and wrist, I immediately relax, sink the left arm, lift the right arm, and cycle it palm upward, from the hip past the left elbow to deliver a blow diagonally to his neck and throat. The opponent will not know what to do. At the same time, the right leg takes a step to the right rear corner. Shift the weight firmly on it to support the power of the right palm. The left toes follow the turn of the waist to the right to support the discharge of the attacker. The left wrist sinks to the left side of the knee in order to keep the balance. If the opponent is hit by my palm he will surely fly out a great distance.

Posture 21

22. Cloudy Hands, Right

If the opponent uses his left arm to move my right palm and his right fist to strike my right chest, I turn my right wrist downward, relax it, and move it in front of my right chest. The left hand follows the waist's turn to the extreme right and stops beside the right hip. The palms face each other. The left foot takes a step straight to the left front to relax the waist, neutralize, and prepare to protect the groin. If the opponent knows his attack is in vain, he will quickly withdraw his fist, to strike my left chest, and kick my groin with his right leg. I relax my left chest, sink my left hip joint, and turn the waist to the extreme left side; the right foot moves inward a half step, pointing straight as in the beginning posture. At the same time, lift the left hand, palm facing inward, and bring it to adhere to the opponent's fist. Move it to the left throat level to neutralize the opponent's force. The right palm drops, following the left palm's turn, and the palms face each other beside the left hip, as on the right side. Let the opponent's kick to the groin be in vain. His hands and feet strike swiftly, but I am moving in a leisurely manner. The name "Cloudy Hands" means I am moving like the floating clouds and running water, from inaction to action. When you exchange the substantial and insubstantial, the waist turns like a mill. Even while turning as if on horseback you must still differentiate substantial and insubstantial. You should not be double-weighted. The two hands follow the turn of the waist along the central axis. The upper palm faces inward at the throat, and the lower palm faces the navel. The trunk is upright as in

Posture 22

the beginning posture. You should never have hollows and projections, continuities and discontinuities. This posture is functionally based on the turning of the waist and hips, which permits you to move the opponent's root and throw him out. Students should carefully study and comprehend this.

23. Cloudy Hands, Left
Cloudy Hands Right, Cloudy Hands Left, and Single Whip. The directions for these postures are given above.

Posture 23

24. Descending Single Whip

From Single Whip—if the opponent uses his right hand to grasp my left palm, I immediately turn out my right toe, and shift my weight onto the right leg. The left toe turns in 45° so that it is straight, and I simultaneously move the left palm back to the front of the left hip. The finger tips point down along the knee and heel and poke forward. The left toes turn back out 90°, and the hooked right hand drops circularly for balance. This thwarts the opponent's grasp. At the same time, my offense is mobilized.

Posture 24

25. Golden Pheasant Stands on One Leg: Right Side

If the opponent uses his left hand to help his right to pull back, I follow him, rising up (from Descending Single Whip), and pointing my right finger tips toward his throat. My right knee rises to strike his groin; my toes point downward. If the opponent yields, then I change, using my toes to kick his groin. It is necessary to bend the left knee to stand stably in this posture. The left hand drops beside the left hip to keep the balance.

Posture 25

26. Golden Pheasant Stands on One Leg: Left Side
This explanation is given in the previous posture.

Posture 26

27. Separate Right Foot

If the opponent grasps my left wrist, I immediately turn it upwards, step back to the left, and sink to the left rear. I lift up the right palm and touch his left elbow as in Rollback. At the same time, the right foot becomes insubstantial and moves a little to the left in front for balance. At that moment, he knows his opportunity is gone, and he stops and moves back. Then I turn the left wrist downward to conceal the pull and help the right hand to Roll Back. I place the left wrist on the right wrist to form the Cross Hands position. If the opponent withdraws his hand to attack again, I separate my right hand, hold his left wrist, and quickly raise the right foot to kick his left knee or left ribs. The foot is extended in one straight line. The eyes focus in the same direction as the right hand, and the left hand and forearm point upward to balance the right arm.

Posture 27

28. Separate Left Foot
The explanation is given above.

Posture 28

29. Turn and Kick with Heel

If the opponent's right hand attacks me directly behind my left rear, I withdraw the left hand and leg and lift the right toes slightly. Fanning with the right forearm, I follow the waist and turn counterclockwise to the rear. When the right wrist touches the left wrist, the left hand separates forward and lightly grasps the opponent's right wrist. The right hand separates to the right rear to keep its balance with the left hand. The left heel delivers a kick to the opponent's groin. The right knee is bent slightly to keep the stability of the form. The eyes focus in the direction of the left hand. The opponent will fall.

Posture 29

Brush Knee, Left
The posture has been previously explained. (See 12th posture).

30. Brush Knee, Right
The posture is like Brush Knee, Left.

Posture 30

31. Step Forward and Strike with Fist

If the opponent kicks with his left leg, I relax my waist and shift my weight to the rear, turn my right toes out, and turn my right hand up to form a fist at the side of my hip joint. The left palm also moves to the right side, by the hip. I shift the weight to the right leg, and step forward with the other leg. I shift the weight to the left. The left hand follows the motion and brushes to the left. The opponent falls down to my right side and my right fist strikes his left waist. This is called *tsai ch'ui* [plant fist].

Step Forward and Wardoff

If the opponent turns his body and attacks me with his left hand, I shift onto my rear leg and turn out my left toe. I then shift my weight onto my left leg, open my right fist and Wardoff upward. The right leg follows, taking a step forward. Then Rollback, Press, Push, and Single Whip follow as in the previous explanation.

Posture 31

32. Fair Lady Weaves at the Shuttle #1

If the opponent strikes from above at the right rear with his right hand, I shift my weight to my rear leg. I turn my front toes clockwise as far as possible and shift the weight onto it. Turn up the left palm and move it under the right armpit. Open the hooked right hand, palm up, and move the right heel back. Take a half step to the right front and shift the weight onto it. Step forward with the left foot to the right rear corner and shift the weight onto it. The left palm follows the right forearm and turns outward to adhere to the opponent's right hand. Under the left elbow, the right palm pushes the opponent's right chest. Extend the right knee slightly to enhance the push. There is no opponent who will not fall down. This posture can change from right to left. "Suddenly appears, suddenly disappears." It adapts to attack any weak point. Therefore, it is named *Y'u N'i Ch'uan So.* This describes the skillfulness and quickness of this posture.

Posture 32

33. Fair Lady Weaves at the Shuttle #2

If the opponent attacks from the right rear, respond as above but changing the direction of the turn. First shift the weight onto the rear leg, and turn clockwise as far as possible, rotating the left toes to follow the waist. The right palm faces upwards and is placed under the left elbow. Turn the body 135° and then shift the weight on to the left leg. The right leg steps 270° to the corner. Shift the weight on it. The rest is as in the previous posture.

Fair Lady Weaves at the Shuttle #3

From the previous posture—shift the weight to the rear leg, turn up the left palm, and place it under the right elbow as above. Then take a left step 90° to the corner. The rest is as above.

Fair Lady Weaves at the Shuttle #4

From the previous posture the right leg takes a step 270° to the corner. The rest is like Fair Lady, number two. Then do Grasp the Sparrow's Tail: (Wardoff, Rollback, Press, Push) Single Whip, and Descending Single Whip. All these are identical to previous descriptions.

Posture 33

34. Step Forward to Seven Stars

The previous posture yields to the opponent's strike with the right hand from above. When the opponent's strike fails, I immediately shift the weight from the left, and the right foot takes a half step forward with the toes touching the ground. At the same time, open the right hooked hand and drop it down to follow the right foot forward. When the right hand is in front of the chest, both hands become fists, the wrists crossed. The fists punch the opponent's chest. This punch is very powerful. When the opponent receives the blow there is great danger he will be gravely injured. Be careful when you use it.

Posture 34

35. Step Back and Ride the Tiger

If the opponent uses two hooked hands to separate my fists and kicks my groin with his right foot, I immediately step back with my right foot and shift the weight onto it. My left foot also moves back a half step with the toes touching the ground and becomes insubstantial. I withdraw my right fist, open the palm, and cycle it to the right rear and forward. The palm stops by the right shoulder, prepared to strike the opponent's right temple. The left fist drops and brushes the knee on the left side to block the opponent's kick and to protect the groin. This modifies the opponent's attack, which is powerful like a tiger. I step back and ride on it.

Posture 35

36. Turn the Body and Sweep the Lotus with Leg

If another opponent attacks me from the rear, and the attacks from the front and rear are each closing in, my right palm suddenly drops across to the left waist to store up power. My left arm moves to the left side to help the body turn. The left foot lifts up slightly. Pivoting on the right toes, simultaneously lift up the left leg, wind up slightly to the left and then turn to the right. To help the body turn 360°, use the left hand and left leg like a tornado to strike the opponent's knee and cheek. Then drop the left leg and shift onto it. The right toes touch the ground. The opponent in front attacks. My palms adhere respectively, to his elbow and wrist. I lift up my right leg and sweep from left to right, hitting his right waist — just like a wind waving the lotus leaves. If you do not relax and sink the waist and hips, the wonderful application will not occur. But this technique is dangerous. Do not use it casually. Be careful!

Posture 36

37. Bend the Bow, Shoot the Tiger

If the opponent withdraws and pushes as a counter-attack, move the right leg back, and put it down to the right front side. The two palms follow the waist, turning to the right rear and circling up. When the right palm reaches the right ear, both palms become fists. The left wrist drops to the side of the left hip to hit the opponent's abdomen. When the right fist reaches the right forehead, it strikes the opponent's left temple. The "tiger's mouth" of the two fists face each other as in bending a bow to shoot the tiger. This posture manifests vigorous defense against a strong opponent.

Step Forward, Deflect Downward, and Punch; Withdraw and Push; Cross Hands are all as described previously.

Posture 37

Ending T'ai Chi

If the opponent uses two fists to attack my two wrists, and uses strong force to press down, I lower my hands to both sides of the hips, and I stand up as in the beginning posture. Then the opponent's power is in vain and he will fall down as if kneeling before me. This posture is the end of the whole set. The practitioner must not neglect it. The Ending of T'ai Chi Ch'uan means the *Liang I, Sze Hsiang, Pa Kua,* and Sixty-Four Hexagrams, all return to *T'ai Chi.* Concentrate the *hsin, I,* and *Ch'i.* All returns to the *tan t'ien.* Gather the spirit and quiet the thinking. It is firm once you know it. Don't lose it. Don't let an expert laugh at you.

Push Hands

The fundamental movements of Push Hands are contained in Grasp the Sparrow's Tail, as described above. In Chapter Eleven, it is said that the Heavenly Level is the function of feeling. Listening to Strength [*t'ing chin*], Interpreting Strength [*tung chin*], and Omnipotence are all based on push hands. It is an orderly progression from *T'ing Chin* to Omnipotence, which is the pinnacle. The practitioner should begin from push hands and practice until mastery is achieved. Then you can gain something. The following pictures are *P'eng, Lu, Chi, An:* Wardoff, Rollback, Press and Push — the four cardinal directions of Push Hands. It applies the principle of giving up yourself to follow others with *chan, lien, t'ieh, sui* of fixed-step Push Hands. *P'eng, Lu, Chi, An* are special terms in the martial arts. These terms are used differently in the *Shuo Wen Chih*, and the meanings are not related. These four postures have been described in the previous section. The photographs are of me and one of my students, Kuo Ch'ing-fang. For the sake of clarity I am A and he is B.

1. Wardoff

Left Wardoff: The position of A's left arm is like an empty embrace; the arm adheres to B's forearm. A sinks on his left leg. This is left Wardoff. The right palm is placed beside the right hip to keep the balance. B's hands and step are just like those of A. The sequence and key point are explained in the picture. This is called Single Push-Hand and is the beginning of learning Push-Hands. The first step is to practice relaxing the hands and arms, then — with the addition of the movements of left and right, forward and backward, up and down — to test the techniques of *chan, lien, tieh, sui*.

Right Wardoff: A's right arm is held in an empty embrace to the right front, palm inward, and adheres to B's right elbow. The left palm facing outward is placed between the chest and elbow. A sinks on his right leg. This is right Wardoff. The meaning of Wardoff is given in Chapter Thirteen. In general, the use of force to ward off others is a great mistake. You must use *chan chin* [adhering to strength] to adhere to B's strength. When you feel B's strength, Ward Off, turn the waist, and neutralize. Let his strength fall into emptiness. Then use "a force of four ounces" to pull and parry. If you can raise and discharge, it is most wonderful.

1. Wardoff

2. Press

A uses right Wardoff and B tries to use *chan chin* to adhere and lift. Then A places his left palm on his right forearm and sinks on his right leg. A's waist and hips push forward at the same time to support the Press, and to advance it forward. This technique arises from A realizing B's desire to adhere and raise; therefore, A presses B. If B neutralizes, then A's press must immediately stop; otherwise, A will doubtless be thrown out. If B does not know how to neutralize and resists, then A first uses *chan chin* to lift B, after which he presses on him. B will then fall out a great distance.

2. Press

3. Rollback

When A uses Press and B neutralizes it, A immediately turns the waist to the right rear and sinks the right elbow. The right wrist moves past B's left elbow and cycles up. A's right elbow adheres to B's left elbow and the back of his left wrist adheres to B's left push. A sits on his rear leg, and his right elbow and left wrist simultaneously turn up slightly to neutralize B's push to the left rear corner until it is negated. This is the correct technique, although it is the most difficult in Push-Hands to use because, if it is not correct, you will rollback the opponent's force into your own body. You will be unable to neutralize, and your opponent will push you out. Because this posture is like opening your door to invite the robbers to come in, its effect is to entice the opponent to enter deeply and to fall into your trap. Then you will catch him. The method is to attempt to snare your opponent without really trying, by not separating and not trying to adhere. Wait for the opportunity, then act. Its wonderful use is limitless.

3. Rollback

4. Push

When A uses Rollback, B will store up the energy
and will not continue to push. Then A's right palm will
push the back of B's right wrist, and A's left palm will
push B's right elbow. A's eyes look forward. The waist
and hips follow the front leg forward to support the
pushing power, causing B to fall. If you do not use this
technique correctly there are three possible results: One,
if you did not get the right opportunity, then B will neutralize the push and you have risked pushing in vain.
Two, if you do not have the right timing then you will
collide with each other and lose control. Three, if you
have neither the opportunity, nor the timing, and, if, at
the same time, you have no listening ability, and you
dare to use force to push, then you will certainly be the
one who will be pushed, far out. Concerning this the
practitioner must study carefully; then he can comprehend it.

4. Push

大
攄 *Ta Lu*

Ta Lu is four-corner Push-Hands. It is the technique
of using *Ts'ai, Lieh, Chou, Kao,* and is equated with
the Four Trigrams: *Chen, Sun, Ken, Tui.* It supports
P'eng, Lu, Chi, An, the four cardinal directions of
Push-Hands, and is limited to the changes of the four
trigrams: *Ch'ien, K'un, K'an, Li.* The *Book of Changes*
fittingly says, "*Yin* and *Yang* mutually rub each other
and the Eight Trigrams mutually succeed each other."
T'ai Chi cannot be separated from *Yin* and *Yang,* the
Eight Trigrams, and the Five Elements. The Five Elements are used mainly in *San Shou* and not here. That
will be explained later. *Ts'ai, Lieh, Chou, K'ao* are
special terms like *P'eng, Lu, Chi, An.* This can be directly explained and you need not relate it to other explanations. *Ts'ai* uses the thumb and middle finger to
hold lightly the opponent's wrist in order to follow his
tendency and send him out. It is like Brush-Knee which
contains *Ts'ai.* With *Lieh,* the opponent pushes my
elbow tightly and I follow his tendency to neutralize,
using the palm to hit the head. It is like White-Crane-
Spreads-Wings and Step-Back-Ride-the-Tiger. *Chou*
means to use the elbow to strike as in Step-Forward-
Deflect-Downward and Hooked-Hands (which hide the
elbow). *K'ao* is to use the shoulder to pursue the opportunity to hit. It is like the use of the Shoulder after Lift-

Hands. The pictures are of me and my classmate Li Shou-chien. There is still separation of A and B as in the previous pictures of Push-Hands. I am A. The application is as follows.

1. *Ta Shou*

When you first touch hands, A and B face each other East-West or North-South. Both Wardoff with the

right arm. The weight shifts to the left leg and both lift up the right leg slightly. Place the left palm similarly to Press posture.

2. Ts'ai

B sinks on his right leg and takes a step to the left front with his left leg. B then immediately moves his right foot to step in between A's legs and uses his shoulder to hit A's lower ribs. A immediately takes a step to

the right rear corner with his right leg. A's left elbow
rolls back B's right elbow and right hand pulls B's right
wrist. This is *Ts'ai*.

3. Lieh

A uses *Ts'ai* on B's wrist, and B neutralizes it. A
immediately uses the right hand to circle upward from
the right rear to hit B's face with the palm. This is *Lieh*.

4. K'ao

When A uses *Lieh*, B immediately uses Wardoff with his right arm and steps back with his right foot to close the step with his left. The left heel rotates to the left 45° and B shifts the weight onto it. The right foot takes a step to the right rear corner and B still uses Rollback to pull A's right wrist. At the same time, A follows B's pull and steps forward with his right foot close to the left step, and sinks on it. A steps to the left front with his

left foot and immediately directs his step in between B's legs with his right leg. A then shoulders B. This is *K'ao*.

5. Chou

B neutralizes A's shoulder and uses *Lieh*. A uses Wardoff with his right arm and hides his elbow waiting for the opportunity to take action. Its wonderful function is unlimited. This is *Chou*.

 *San Shou*

San Shou means free fighting. There is no definite method to it. Both *T'ui shou* [Push Hands] and *Ta Lu* issue from familiarity with the correct touch. From familiarity with the correct touch you will learn to *t'ing chin* [listen to strength]. After learning *t'ing chin*, you will gradually comprehend *tung chin* [understanding strength]. After comprehending *tung chin*, nothing any longer seems touched or not touched, scattered or not scattered, adhered to or not adhered to, followed or not followed. All are unnecessary explanations. They do not touch on the main point. The way of *San Shou* is located in the Five Elements and called *chin, t'ui, ku, pan, ting*. If you can *tung chin* and know the technique, then the application is complete. I followed Professor Yang for seven years and only one *chin* was difficult to learn. It was *chieh chin* [receiving *chin*]. If your achievement reaches this level, then you do not have to worry about the other kinds of *chin*. The explanation of *chieh chin* is found through the analogy of someone throwing a ball to hit me. If I resist the ball or hit it, it will bounce out. This is the *chin* of colliding and is not *chieh chin*. If the ball is light, it will be easy to bounce it out. However, if the ball's weight is several hundred pounds, how can I bounce it out? Hence, colliding is not correct. You must attract it and then toss it out. This is *chieh chin*. If the ball is moving slow or fast, or is light or heavy it is still the same. *Chan* [adhere], *t'ing* [listen], *t'i* [raise], *fang* [discharge] are all in it. Combine attraction and discharge almost simultaneously. The power is intensified in a very small space. This almost attains the highest wisdom in which *San Shou* becomes meaningless. Therefore, I say nothing can replace T'ai Chi Ch'uan. It is the supreme. Besides *chieh chin* there is nothing else.

Cheng Tzu's
Thirteen Treatises
on T'ai Chi Ch'uan

Section III

Answers to
Students' Questions

I. Concerning Chang San-Feng's
T'ai Chi Ch'uan Lun

Question 1: If the *ch'i* is stimulated and the *shen* is internally gathered, does it mean that the *hsin* mobilizes the *ch'i* and the *ch'i* mobilizes the body? Is this the origin of the inner and the outer mutually responding to each other and also the unification of movement and stillness? Please explain.

Answer: Your question is good. To mobilize the *ch'i* throughout the body is the basis of the internal. Stimulating the *ch'i* is the end result and is external. Gathering internally is stillness and stimulating the *ch'i* is motion. They are mutually responsive and joined together. To excite the *ch'i* means not only to stimulate one's own *ch'i* but to join one's *ch'i* to the *ch'i* of Nature so as to reinforce each other. Then it is excellent.

Question 2: "Let the postures be without breaks or holes, hollows or projection, or discontinuities and continuities of form." Does this quotation have the same meaning as the description from the Treatise "Strength and Physics" which says, "Slowly without breaks, circularly and continuously repeating itself, wonderful and divine, without end"?

Answer: Yes, but it is not as clear and obvious as the statement from the T'ai Chi *Classics* that says, "Stand like a balance, rotate actively like a wheel."

Question 3: "The motion should be rooted in the feet, released through the legs, controlled by the waist, and manifested through the fingers." The theory and the details have already been clearly explained in Treatise Eleven, Human Level, second and third degree. What is the method of mobilizing the hands and feet at the same time?

Answer: This is an excellent question. Here it is said, "It is rooted in the feet and manifested in the fingers." The *chin* is strung together and it is clearly shown in the substance and application. When you discharge the opponent it can be seen as the *ch'i* arriving. The root can never be dislodged. So you must make the right leg coordinate with the left hand and the left leg coordinate with the right hand. This is called "strung together."

Question 4: When the opportunity and the timing are correct it is the pinnacle of *tung chin*. This is clearly explained in your Treatise Eleven, Heaven Level, second degree, but to know its application is difficult. Please give some examples.

Answer: Study my commentary on the ninth point in the last treatise of the Thirteen Treatises and you will find it.

Question 5: After I read Treatise Seven on "Strength and Physics" concerning the use of leverage I understood the

quote, "Up or down, front or back, left or right. . . . " Is there anymore?
Answer: Just change the position and think about it. The substance and the application are similar.

Question 6: "By alternation of the force of pulling and pushing, the root is severed and the object is quickly toppled, without a doubt." Is that *t'i chin*?
Answer: To lift up is *t'i chin*, but this is not the power capable of raising up an opponent. That power comes by first pulling and then pushing, meaning that you first give way before you attain it. It is similar to squatting down first to get the power for jumping up. In physics, the equation is Force × Speed × Time = Energy.

Question 7: "In motion it separates; in stillness they fuse." What is the difference between separating and fusing, bending and extending, and opening and closing?
Answer: With regards to T'ai Chi, in stillness it fuses and in motion it separates. However, opening and closing refer to the body and the *ch'i*. When the body opens, the *ch'i* closes, and vice versa. Bending and extending is the same as opening and closing.

II. Concerning Wang Ts'ung-yueh's T'ai Chi Ch'uan Lun

Question 1: "When the opponent is hard and I am supple, it is called *tsou* (yielding). When I follow the opponent and he becomes backed up, it is called *nien* (adherence)." I already know the application of *kang* (hard) and *jou* (supple). What are *shun, pei* and *nien*?

Answer: *Shun* is called "giving yourself up to follow others;" likewise: 'If others don't move, I don't move." Then others cannot figure me out. If I give others a gap, this is called *pei*. "If others move slightly, I move first:" means I know others have a gap and then to take advantage of it, I become first and others fall behind—this is also called *pei*. It is all based on *t'ing chin* (listening to strength), so that you must have *nien*.

Question 2: "From familiarity with the correct touch, one gradually comprehends *chin* (internal force); from the comprehension of *chin* one can reach wisdom" is all clearly explained in Treatise Eleven, Heaven Level, second and third degree. Besides this explanation, is there anything else?
Answer: It is complete. There is nothing else.

Question 3: "Empty the left whenever a pressure appears, and similarly the right." What does this mean?
Answer: This is the way to use it. If the opponent gives me a hearty push on my left, I empty my left side—similarly from the right. *Ao* means empty. In the substance it occurs in different ways.

Question 4: What does it mean to say, "(So light an object as) a feather cannot be placed and (so small an insect as) a fly cannot alight"?
Answer: During Push-Hands, besides *chan* and *lien* (adherence), the opponent will try to put his strength on me. I cannot receive even the weight of a feather or the motion of a fly.

III. Concerning Wu Yu Hsiang's Exposition of Insights Into the Practice of the Thirteen Postures

Question 1: What is the difference between, on the one hand, "The *hsin* (mind) mobilizes the *ch'i* (breath). Make the *ch'i* sink calmly; then it gathers and permeates the bones;" and, on the other hand, both "The *shen* (spirit) should be internally gathered" and "The *ch'i* sticks to the back and permeates the spine"?

Answer: The word "gather" is the same, but *shen* and *ch'i* are different. When the *shen* is gathered the mind becomes clear. When the *ch'i* is gathered in the bone, it becomes the basis of another condition about which there are ample quotes: "If there is no *ch'i* there is pure hardness;" and "The mobilization of the *chin* (internal strength) is like refining steel a hundred times over."

Question 2: "To *fa chin* (release energy), sink, and relax completely." Why is someone still required to relax when he executes *fa chin*?

Answer: "To sink" is the substance and depends on me; "to relax" is the application and is connected with others. When you discharge others, it is like cleanly releasing an arrow from a bowstring.

Question 3: "The *li* (force) is released by the back, and the steps follow the changes of the body." Is this the same *li* that is mentioned in Treatise Six, which circulates through the *jen* and *tu* meridians? Are "the steps following the changes of the body" commanded by the waist?

Answer: The word *li* in the sentence "the *li* released by the back" should be *chin*. The phrase "released by the back" means force originating in the back. Therefore, the statements "Store up the *chin* (internal strength) like drawing a bow," "The steps following the changes of the body," and "Commanded by the waist" are all correct.

Question 4: "To withdraw is then to release, to release is to withdraw. In discontinuity there is still continuity." The "withdraw" already contains the meaning "to *t'i fang*," but what is "in discontinuity there is still continuity"? **Answer:** Discontinuity is the physical form and continuity is the *i* (mind). It is like a broken lotus root with the fibers still connected. In Chinese calligraphy the stroke may be broken, but the mind is still connected.

Question 5: "In advancing and returning there must be folding. Going forward and back there must be changes." Please elaborate on these two sentences.
Answer: It is said that the folding technique is the secret of the Yang family. It is to fold the three parts: the shoulder, the elbow and the wrist. The technique is strengthened by unlimited repetitions and changes of going forward and back.

Question 6: "Throughout the body, the *i* (mind) relies on the *ching shen* (spirit), not on the *ch'i* (breath). If it relied on the *ch'i* it would become stagnant. If there is *ch'i*, there is no *li* (external strength). If there is no *ch'i*, there is pure steel." In the beginning when I read this I doubted it. I later studied Treatise Eleven, Heaven Level, third degree and completely understood it. Besides this, is there any further explanation?
Answer: There is none.

214

IV. Concerning the Song of Thirteen Postures

Question 1: "Being still, when attacked by the opponent, be tranquil and move in stillness; (my) changes caused by the opponent fill him with wonder. Be still and wait for motion, for in motion there is also stillness." Why is it said "fill him with wonder"?

Answer: If you are not still, you cannot perceive your opponent's changes. Let him change but you can still control him with stillness. That is what "fill him with wonder" means.

Question 2: Is the sentence, "Completely relax the abdomen and the *ch'i* (breath) rises up" the same as the statement in Treatise Eleven, Earth Level, third degree, "The *tan t'ien* mobilizes the *ch'i*"?

Answer: No. The latter is the function of the exhalation when you *fa chin*. When you *fa chin* you cannot hold your breath. If you do you will be internally injured. Therefore you must give a loud shout; then the *ch'i* follows the *chin* rising up.

V. Concerning the Song of Push Hands

Question 1: In the sentence, "Be conscientious in *p'eng* (ward-off), *lu* (rollback), *chi* (press), and *an* (push)," what does conscientious really mean?

Answer: It has already been explained in the commentary in Treatise Thirteen, number eleven.

Question 2: The sentence, "Use four ounces to deflect a thousand pounds" has been already clearly explained in the Treatise Thirteen, number twelve. Besides this is

there any further explanation?
Answer: No.

Question 3: "Attract to emptiness, absorb, and discharge; attach (*chan, lien, t'ieh, sui*) without *tiu ting* (losing) the attachment." Does "absorb" mean to store up the energy and then release and what does "without *tiu ting* (losing) the attachment" mean?
Answer: This is also explained by *ti fang*. *Tiu* is really disconnecting. *Ting* means contrary force. These two words are contrary to *lien* and *sui*. Because you have yourself, you cannot give yourself up to follow others.

Song of Substance and Function

T'ai Chi Ch'uan.

Thirteen postures.

The marvel lies in the two *ch'i* divided into *Yin* and *Yang*.

It transforms the myriad and returns to the One.

Returns to the One.

T'ai Chi Ch'uan.

The *Liang I* (Two Primordial Powers) and the *Sze Hsiang* (Four Manifestations) are chaos and boundless.

To ride the winds how about suspending the headtop?

I have some words to reveal now to those who can know.

If the *yung ch'uan* (bubbling well) has no root and the waist has no commander, studying hard till death will be of no help.

The form and function are mutually connected
and nothing more.

The *hao jan chih ch'i* (Great *Ch'i*)
can be conducted to the hand.

Wardoff, rollback,
press, push
pull, split
elbow, shoulder.

Step forward, step back,
look left, look right,
central equilibrium.

Not neutralizing it naturally neutralizes,
not yielding it naturally yields.

(When) the foot wants to advance
first shift backwards.

The body is like a floating cloud.

In push-hands the hands are not needed.

The whole body is a hand
and the hand is not a hand.

But the mind must stay
in the place it should be.

The T'ai Chi Ch'uan Classics, which comprise the second half
of Section III, have already been translated in another book,
The Essence of T'ai Chi Ch'uan.

Glossary

Bubbling Well: *Yung ch'uan*. The center of the foot where the root lies. It corresponds to the first point on the kidney meridian.

Chan Kung: Standing practice which helps to develop the legs, root, *ch'i* and relaxation.

Chan, Lien, Tieh, Sui, Pu Tiu pu Ting: This refers to the sticking aspect or adherence in T'ai Chi Ch'uan. *Chan* and *lien* are vertical adhering movements, lifting from above and supporting from below, respectively. *T'ieh* is adherence in horizontal motion, and *sui* is adherence from the rear. *Pu tiu pu ting* means to not lose the adherence or to resist.

Ch'i: Breath or breath energy. The *ch'i* one is born with or receives from one's parents is called pre-natal *ch'i*. After birth one begins to consume this *ch'i*, replacing it (incompletely) with *ch'i* derived from food or air. This is called post-natal *ch'i*. Any metabolic or psychospiritual transformation of energy may be characterized as *ch'i*.

Ch'i Hai: Sea of *ch'i* or *tan t'ien*. Located in the abdomen, this point is critical for the development of the *ch'i*. It corresponds to the sixth point on the *jen* channel of the body.

Ch'ien, Po, Ts'ai, Chou: Lead, parry, pull, and elbow are four techniques within the Rollback posture.

Chin: One of the main objectives of T'ai Chi Ch'uan is the development of *chin* or internal force. *Chin* is contrasted with *li*, which refers to muscular contraction and release. *Chin* is said to generate its power from the sinews rather than from the muscles binding together and striking with the bones. *Chin* is developed through circular changes while the flexations of *li* follow straight lines.

Chin, T'ui, Ku, Pan, Ting: These are some of the original

thirteen postures of T'ai Chi Ch'uan and translatable as: step forward, step back, look left, look right, and central equilibrium.

Ching: This refers to the seminal essence developed from the kidney *ch'i* of the body.

Ching Shen: Spirit—having almost exactly the same connotations as in English.

Chung Ting: Central equilibrium, see *chin, t'ui, ku, pan, ting*. It means being centrally balanced and firmly rooted.

Fa Chin: To release the internal force (*chin*).

Grasp Sparrow's Tail: A series of four postures (Wardoff, Rollback, Press, Push) which form the basis of the solo movements.

Hsiang: see *sze hsiang*.

Hu K'ou: Tiger's mouth—the space located between the index finger and the thumb of the hand.

Huang Ti: The Yellow Emperor. A mythological figure of Ancient China who wrote the *Nei Ching* or *The Yellow Emperor's Classic of Internal Medicine*. This *Classic* is the contemporary basis of Chinese traditional medicine.

I: Mind. *I* and *ch'i* are separate concepts but are almost inseparable in function. One of the objectives of T'ai Chi Ch'uan is to make the *ch'i*, or breath-energy, follow the dictates of the *i* through an initial sinking of the *ch'i* to the *tan t'ien*.

Jen Mai: The *jen mai* is sometimes referred to as the conception vessel in traditional Chinese medicine and corresponds to the midline travelling up the front of the body. It is classified as one of the extra meridians of the body.

K'ung Ming (also known as Chu Ko-liang): A famous statesman of ancient China during the Three Kingdoms Period.

Lao Kung: This refers to the eighth point on the pericardium meridian which is located on the middle of the palm of the hand. It is an important junction for the *ch'i* to pass through before it travels to the fingers.

Li: Using the muscles to bind the bones together into a rigid forceful matrix. This style of strike or push is antithetical to the techniques of T'ai Chi Ch'uan. See *chin*.

Liang I: Two Primordial Powers, i.e., Heaven and Earth, *Yin* and *Yang* (the cosmological forces creating all things). The *Liang I* evolved from *T'ai Chi* and is symbolized in the *Book of Changes* by a broken, then an unbroken line. From these representations the *Sze Hsiang* evolved and then the eight trigrams. (See: *Pa Kua* and *Sze Hsiang*.)

Lieh: This is one of the basic thirteen postures of the T'ai Chi Ch'uan movements—striking the opponent with an open palm.

Ming Men: This is an acupuncture point located between the third and fourth lumbar vertebrae of the spine and closely associated with the prenatal kidney *ch'i*.

Mo Tzu: A philosopher of the Warring States Period in ancient China.

Ni Wan: A point located on the midline at the top of the head.

Pa Kua: Literally, eight trigrams. The trigrams consist of all the combinations of broken and unbroken lines (binary system) in three positions, as follows:

☰ *Ch'ien*   ☷ *K'un*   ☵ *K'an*   ☲ *Li*

☳ *Chen*   ☴ *Sun*   ☶ *Ken*   ☱ *Tui*

P'eng Chu (also known as Yueh Fei): A noted general of the Sung Dynasty.

Seven Emotions: anger, joy, sorrow, fright, fear, thinking, worry.

Shen: Spirit. See *ching shen*.

Shuo Wen Chieh Chih: An ancient Chinese dictionary.

Six Desires: This is a Buddhist term which refers to the six sexual attractions rising from color, form, carriage, voice, smoothness, and features.

Sixty-Four Hexagrams: These are the various pairings of the eight trigrams which represent the coming together of Heaven and Earth, or the *Yin* and *Yang*, as they interact and affect human affairs. Refer to the *Book of Changes* (*I Ching*).

Three Gates: These refer to the sacral and occipital regions and the top of the head, the three areas of the body which correspond to the Western parasympathetic nerves and through which the *ch'i* must circulate in order for the practitioner to achieve the highest levels of practice in T'ai Chi Ch'uan.

Sze Hsiang: Four Manifestations. Four diagrams denoting the evolution of the cosmos from *Yin* and *Yang* to the eight trigrams.

Yin I   *Yang I*

T'ai Yin   Hsiao Yang   *Hsiao Yin   T'ai Yang*

T'i Chin: Uprooting strength.

T'i Ho: Raise and bring together.

Ting Chin: This is the ability to be rooted and immovable as opposed to being hard and resistant to the opponent's attack.

T'ing Chin: Listening to the opponent's strength.

Tu Mai: One of those classified among the Eight Extra Meridians of the body, it travels up the midline of the back, the back of the head, to the top of the head, and down the front of the face to the upper lip.

Tung Chin; Interpreting the opponent's strength. This represents one of the most refined levels of push-hands practice. The practitioner at this level must be able to distinguish between the real or the feint; the solid or the hollow; the big or the little; the longer reach or the shorter; the rigid or the pliable; and the differentiation of "inner pliable strength" and "outer rigid force."